What is Theology?

MAURICE WILES

What is Theology?

OXFORD UNIVERSITY PRESS

LONDON   OXFORD   NEW YORK

1976

Oxford University Press, Walton Street, Oxford OX2 6DP

LONDON OXFORD GLASGOW NEW YORK
TORONTO MELBOURNE WELLINGTON CAPE TOWN
IBADAN NAIROBI DAR ES SALAAM LUSAKA ADDIS ABABA
KUALA LUMPUR SINGAPORE JAKARTA HONG KONG TOKYO
DELHI BOMBAY CALCUTTA MADRAS KARACHI

Paperback ISBN 0 19 289066 2
Case-bound ISBN 0 19 213525 2

*First published in the Oxford Paperbacks University Series 1976 and
simultaneously in a cloth bound edition*

Printed in Great Britain by
Thomson Litho Ltd., East Kilbride, Scotland.

Contents

Preface

This book is based on lectures which have been given in various forms over a number of years to students embarking on the study of Christian theology at King's College, London, on the Southwark Ordination Course and in the University of Oxford.

It does not aim to provide a basic account of Christian faith or an outline sketch of Christian theology. It is a discussion of the issues that arise when one tries to reflect on what is involved in doing theology. Such reflection is incumbent upon theologians, but will, I hope, be of interest also to those who are not theologians themselves but who want to know how a theologian understands his discipline.

I have kept very close to the form and style of the original lectures. Those were given to people about to start on a course of theological study. My aim was not only to give some idea of what the various parts of that course were like in themselves, but still more to give some idea of how they fitted together into a coherent whole. And I wanted to do that in a way which would convey the worthwhileness and the excitement of the subject.

I have not therefore tried to be comprehensive. There are other things that can be said about theology that I have not touched upon. But I have tried to select what seem to me the central issues. Nor have I developed the issues that I have raised in a systematic way. I have tried rather to put the main point as succinctly as I can and to use specific illustrations to convey an idea of the types of problem and of the possibilities that are involved. But theology is done in many different ways. I have tried to represent something of that variety, but in this respect too have made no attempt to be comprehensive. In the last analysis what I have written is an account of theology as I myself believe it should be done.

The book falls into two main parts. In the first I have described how the main sections of theological study are tackled. In the second I have discussed the implications of other disciplines for the study of theology. Thus the two parts of the book come at the same problems from different angles. In both cases I have been rigorously selective. Thus I have included church history and philosophy of religion but not ethics or liturgy in the first half, and sociology but not anthropology in the second. Some selection was inevitable. I hope that by restricting the areas covered, the main issues will stand out more clearly.

Finally, this is a book about Christian theology and not about religious studies. I have tried to say briefly how I understand the relation between the two on pp. 10–13.

Keith Thomas, the editor of the series, Peter Baelz and Morna Hooker all read an earlier draft of this book and made many valuable suggestions. I am extremely grateful to them for their generous help. They are not to be blamed for the many imperfections that remain.

MAURICE WILES

I

Introduction

Some years ago a young Australian arrived to begin theological study in the University of Wales. When asked his intended subject his reply was too quiet to be clearly audible and he found himself enrolled in courses for geology. Too shy to point out the error, he persevered and ended up with a first-class degree in geology. That was no small achievement. For however similar geology and theology may be in sound, they are vastly different in method of study. The word 'geology' derives from two Greek words—'gē' (earth) and 'logos' ('word' or 'reason'). Geology is reasoned discourse about earth. Theology comes similarly from the words 'theos' (God) and 'logos'; it is reasoned discourse about God.

Now the basic method of study in geology is straightforward enough. You get hold of bits of earth, perform various experimental tests upon them and on the basis of those tests build up your understanding of the formation and fundamental properties of the earth. The geologist may in practice seek a good deal of his information from books. But the use of books is essentially secondary. It is an acknowledged short cut. They are of use only in so far as they embody the outcome of earlier experimental work and reflection upon it. It is the experimental work on the earth itself that is basic. But the theologian cannot imitate the geologist's method. For if God be the basic concern of the theologian's study, then his subject matter is not available to him in the way that the geologist's is.

The theologian is not alone in his difficulties, even though they impinge upon him in a specially acute form. There are other disciplines where the appropriate subject-matter is not as directly available as it is for the geologist. If the subject-matter of history is the past, it is not as immediately accessible to the historian as the geologist's subject-matter is to him. He cannot recall the past and examine it in the ways of his own choosing. It is even conceivable that someone should deny the existence of the past at all. Philip Henry Gosse, for example, the eminent geologist who was also a fundamentalist Plymouth Brother, believed that the world was created in 4004 B.C. with all the fossils embedded in the newly-formed rocks, arguing that this was the only way in which an organic universe of the kind we know could have been created at a particular moment in time. For him, therefore, anyone claiming to study the prehistoric past was in fact studying a non-existent subject. But while such a view is logically possible, anyone holding it would be regarded as utterly eccentric and unreasonable. But in the case of God there are many people who are neither eccentric nor unreasonable who deny the existence of any reality corresponding to that word. Theology in their view has no subject matter.

Is it then possible to develop reasoned discourse about a subject whose very existence is denied by some eminently reasonable men? It is a part of the purpose of this book to argue that it is. But at the outset we must acknowledge that, even if that argument is successful, the elusiveness of its essential subject-matter gives to theology a highly problematical character.

Theologians sometimes try to evade the full force of this embarrassing fact. There are two contrasting ways in which they may do so.

One way is to accept without demur that there are many people for whom theology is a meaningless subject, but to claim that there is nothing surprising or embarrassing in that. Theology is a 'confessional' subject, intelligible to believers but not to others. Music is similarly incomprehensible to the deaf and art to the blind. So too will theology inevitably be to the unbeliever, but that is evidence of something unsatisfactory in the state of the unbeliever not in the subject-matter of theology. The logic of such a position is to restrict work in theology to believers. They alone will be in a proper position to undertake it. It was indeed not until this century that Oxford University allowed anyone other than a priest of the Church of England to be an examiner in the Honour School of Theology. Within such a confessional range, it would be claimed, there is agreement about the basic subject-matter of theology and the possibility of reasoned discourse about it comparable with that which characterizes other disciplines.

This way of dealing with the difficulty is not dead but it is less common than it used to be. The alternative approach involves a move in precisely the opposite direction. It denies that there are people for whom theology is a meaningless subject. It claims that, whatever people may say, everybody does in fact have some sort of belief in God. A fairly recent example of a move in this direction is a famous passage from one of Paul Tillich's sermons:

The name of this infinite and inexhaustible depth and ground of all being is *God*. That depth is what the word *God* means. And if that word has no such meaning for you, translate it, and speak of the depths of your life, of the source of your being, of your ultimate concern, of what you take seriously without any reservation. Perhaps, in order to do so, you must forget everything traditional that you have learned about God, perhaps even that word itself. For if you know that God means depth, you know much about him. You cannot then call yourself an atheist or unbeliever. For you cannot think or say: Life has no depth! Life is shallow. Being itself is surface only. If you could say this in complete seriousness, you would be an atheist; but otherwise you are not. He who knows about depth knows about God.[1]

But this is not just a modern apologetic device. The same point can be illustrated from the writings of Martin Luther:

What is it to have a God or what is God? As I have often said, the confidence and faith of the heart alone make both God and an idol . . . For the two, faith and God, have inevitable connections.

---

[1] P. Tillich, *Shaking of the Foundations* (London, 1962), pp. 63–4. The quotation is used in this way by J.A.T. Robinson, *Honest to God* (London, 1963), p. 22.

Now, I say, whatever your heart clings to and confides in that is really your God.[1]

On this approach then everyone has a god and everyone must therefore recognize that there is a valid subject-matter for theology to deal with.

Now both these approaches have some force, but neither provides a way of escape from the basic dilemma. It is true that there are many fields of study where there is need for a period of sustained and sympathetic experience before one can judge with any confidence whether there is a real subject to be studied. Freud used to claim that no-one was in a position to assess the validity of psycho-analysis as a way of knowledge unless he had himself undergone the experience of being psycho-analysed. So theology can very properly ask of its critics a readiness to put themselves in the way of the kind of experiences with which it purports to deal. But it must take seriously the reaction of those who do so and still find themselves unconvinced thereby of any reality of God. Theology cannot be content to regard itself simply as the private concern of a group of believers who happen to have had experiences of a particular kind.

Similarly it is true that Marxists or humanists may have some overriding concern which gives unity of meaning and driving force to their lives and which fulfils a rôle very similar to that played by faith in God in the life of the believer. But there are others who lack any such unifying concern—or whose concerns are of a trivial kind. Theology is not just a psychological description of what men's basic convictions happen to be. It claims to be concerned with what ought to be the basic conviction of every man. And if it is to stick to that sort of claim, it cannot avoid acknowledging the elusiveness of its proper subject-matter.

Neither of these two lines of reflection, therefore, offers any real way of escape from the difficulty we have posed. But it might be claimed that the difficulty has arisen because we have too readily accepted the etymology of the word

---

[1] M. Luther, *Large Catechism*, First Part, The First Commandment (cited by G. D. Kaufman, *Systematic Theology* (New York, 1968), p. 21).

'theology' as a guide to its real subject-matter, and that once we allow that assumption to be called in question the difficulty may turn out to be more formal than real. The past may in one sense be the subject-matter of the historian's study, but no working historian is worried by metaphysical doubts about the past's existence or about his inability to travel backwards in time and experience the period of his study at first hand. He still has an accessible and definable subject-matter to study. What he studies are the records of the past. Books (which are of course only one form of such records) play a very different rôle in the work of the historian from that which they play in the work of the geologist. So, it may be claimed, the theologian has an accessible and definite subject-matter in the form of the 'holy books' that he studies. And for the Christian theologian that means the Bible. The work of Christian theology would then be to provide a coherent account of the teaching of the Bible. Now biblical studies certainly have a vitally important place in the work of the Christian theologian. That will be discussed later. But however important that place, the Bible cannot provide a definition of the subject-matter of theology as a whole. Two fundamental reasons why it cannot may be briefly and rather baldly stated. In the first instance it is clear that there is no such thing as 'a coherent account of the teaching of the Bible' which does not draw its criteria of coherence from outside the Bible itself. Not only are there obvious differences of belief between Old and New Testaments, but also within the New Testament itself. And secondly, even in so far as there is a coherent unity of biblical teaching, that cannot simply be taken over as it stands and treated as the end product of the work of theology. The biblical writers share various cultural assumptions characteristic of the ancient world which are alien to almost any modern world-view. The theologian cannot simply be committed in advance to belief in demonic possession or apocalyptic expectations of the kind that underlie St. Mark's gospel and much other New Testament writing besides. Some form of interpretation is called for, and once again the criteria for that interpretative task are not provided by the

Bible itself. Theology must involve something more than simply study of the ancient documents. One has only to recall the immensely varied and erratic views propounded by different sects all claiming to base themselves solely on the teaching of the Bible to recognize how important it is that that 'something more' be brought out fully into the open as an explicit element of critical theological work.

If then theology is a contemporary study, concerned not merely with what has happened and been believed in the past but with what is happening and to be believed now, perhaps the theologian would do better to look for a model to the work of the sociologist rather than to that of the historian. His subject matter could be seen as the documents and life of the community of faith and his task that of the critical interpreter of them. Once again such work is clearly an important part of the theologian's job, but it cannot serve as a complete definition of it. In the first place 'the community of faith' is not a clearly defined entity. Some Roman Catholics before the second Vatican Council might have wished to identify it simply and directly with the Roman Catholic Church, but there is hardly anyone who would want to make any comparable claim today. Moreover theology is not simply a descriptive science. It is not content simply to give an account of the beliefs and practices of Christians, as a sociologist might, for example, of the flat-earth society, without raising questions of the truth or falsity of those beliefs, the appropriateness or inappropriateness of the practices. Indeed all the varying communities of faith claim that their beliefs and practices are in some sense guided by the Bible and those claims call for critical examination.

Thus even when the attempt is made to define the subject-matter of theology in terms of that which is more directly accessible to study—the documents and lives that have formed and at present constitute the communities of believers—there is even at this level a considerable degree of complexity and of elusiveness.

Much of the theologian's time will be taken up with historical and sociological studies of what has been believed in the past and what is believed now, but he cannot abandon his concern with the truth or falsity of those beliefs. His ultimate concern is with God and he must accept the peculiar difficulties that that fact imposes upon him in the prosecution of his studies.

2. FAITH AND THE THEOLOGIAN

Theology, I have argued, cannot be content with a ghetto existence. It is not an esoteric subject intelligible only to a select group of believers. But even if it aims to be intelligible to all, should it equally welcome all men as its practitioners? Most theologians are practising members of the religion whose theology they study. But is this a necessary or a contingent fact? Is faith a prerequisite for the proper prosecution of the theologian's task? And whatever the answer to that question, we still need to ask about the relation between the believing theologian's faith and his theological work.

Theology is parasitic upon religion. If there were no religious faith, there would be no theology. It would therefore be absurd to suggest that there is not or should not be a close connexion between faith and theology. Moreover it is grossly misleading to suggest that an attitude of no faith represents a desirable position of neutrality. Absence of faith arises either from lack of interest in or attention to the subject (and it is difficult to regard that as an essential precondition for being a good scholar of the subject) or else it represents one particular standpoint comparable with the standpoint of faith.

The problem here is one which arises in relation to any study dealing with matters of profound human concern. Someone who is thoroughly uninterested in political affairs is unlikely to make a good political scientist. But nor on the other hand is the most passionately committed party politician. Professor Broad has given expression to this dilemma in an entertaining autobiographical comment in the preface to his book, *Five Types of Ethical Theory*. He writes:

It is perhaps fair to warn the reader that my range of experience, both practical and emotional, is rather exceptionally narrow even for a don. Fellows of Colleges, in Cambridge at any rate, have few temptations to heroic virtue or spectacular vice; and I could wish that the rest of mankind were as fortunately situated. Moreover, I find it difficult to excite myself very much over right and wrong in practice. I have, e.g., no clear idea of what people have in mind when they say that they labour under a sense of sin; yet I do not doubt that, in some cases, this is a genuine experience, which seems vitally important to those who have it, and may really be of profound ethical and metaphysical significance. I recognise that these practical and emotional limitations may make me blind to certain important aspects of moral experience. Still, people who feel very strongly about any subject are liable to over-estimate its importance in the scheme of things. A healthy appetite for righteousness, kept in due control by good manners, is an excellent thing; but to 'hunger and thirst after' it is often merely a symptom of spiritual diabetes. And a white-heat of moral enthusiasm is not perhaps the most favourable condition in which to conduct the analysis of ethical concepts or the criticism of ethical theories. So, having thus given fair warning to my readers, I may at least claim the qualities of my defects.[1]

The general point might be put something like this. Where there is not enough love, there is likely to be a lack of penetration into the inwardness of the subject studied. But too much love may blind a man and prevent him from seeing some of the inherent problems and difficulties. If we apply this principle to theology we may say first that where there is no inkling of faith whatever, there is likely to be a lack of sensitivity towards the issues at stake. This does not mean that every unbeliever is automatically ruled out from the possibility of having such insight, but that there is likely to be a difference between the unbeliever who has never felt the temptation to believe and one who has, however successfully he may have resisted it. But on the other hand too fanatical a faith is equally unlikely to contribute to the making of a good theologian. Does it follow then that the best theologian will be the lukewarm Laodicean Christian?[2] That conclusion would only follow if faith were a simple, straightforward thing, which varied only quantitatively. But

[1] C. D. Broad, *Five Types of Ethical Theory* (London, 1944), pp. xxiv–v.
[2] Cf. Rev. 3:16.

it is not. It may vary qualitatively. It is not just a matter of how much faith a man has but of how he has it. What is called for in the theologian who is also a man of faith, is not that he should have less faith, but that his faith should co-exist with a certain capacity for detachment. This is not an easy thing to achieve, nor is it without its dangers. No-one can be a good art critic without a basic enjoyment of art; but the regular exercise of his critical faculties in a professional manner may have the result of dulling the edge of his capacity for enjoyment, though it need not do so. The marriage expert who is continually involved in analyzing the marriage breakdowns of others may find it more difficult to remain spontaneous in the living of his own married life, but not all marriage experts are thereby doomed to end up in the divorce courts. The combination of faith and critical detachment is a difficult but a possible rôle. It is also a very necessary one, for uncritical religion is a dangerous phenomenon.

But for the Christian theologian there is a further problem. He is committed not only to the general conviction that Christianity is a good thing; he is apparently committed to certain more specific claims. The creeds, for example, speak of the Virgin birth of Christ and of his resurrection. Is it possible to combine particular beliefs of this kind with an appropriate openness of approach to the difficult philosophical and historical questions which those beliefs pose? Reflecting on the past history of the Church suggests the need for caution in the making of any claim that specific beliefs are absolutely essential and irreformable for Christian faith. Not infrequently in the past the beliefs about which such claims have been made by one generation have been treated as less central or have been significantly modified by the next. Nevertheless it would be equally unsatisfactory to suggest that all the items of Christian belief might turn out to be in error without any undermining of Christian faith as a whole. But at this point of our enquiry we must be content simply to note that the believing theologian will meet with tensions between his faith and his study. They are a part of the difficulty of his rôle. But we must look more carefully at the nature and the methods of his work as theologian, before we

are in a position to assess how acute those tensions are and
whether they can effectively be met.

3. RELIGION, RELIGIONS, AND CHRISTIAN THEOLOGY

So far I have been speaking of belief and Christian belief as
if they were one and the same thing, as if the choice were
simply between being a Christian and being an unbeliever.
That is indeed how the situation has appeared to many
Christians in the course of Christian history. But whatever
may be said in explanation of such an attitude in the past,
it is today without justification. Other religions are not
demonic perversions of the true, nor curious survivals from
the past; some of them too are living faiths. Christianity is a
religion among the religions of the world. The claim is sometimes made that Christianity is not a religion, because
religions are human constructs and Christianity is a God-
given faith; but that is an illegitimate attempt to solve a
complex problem in one's own favour by the simple process
of an arbitrary definition. The Christian theologian has to
ask about the relation of his study to the study of other
religions. Can Christian theology constitute a separate study
in its own right? And if it can, what place should be given
within it to the study of religion in general and of other
religions in particular?

The initial impact of these questions on the Christian
theologian may give rise to either of two apparently opposing
reactions. It may underline for him the widespread character
of religious experience and practice and so strengthen his
confidence in the reality, however elusive, of his subject-
matter. Alternatively and more commonly the placing of
other religions alongside Christianity may pose serious problems for him about the truth claims of Christian theology at
the many points at which they are in conflict with the
affirmations of other faiths. More careful study is likely to
qualify any extreme reaction in either direction.

Almost all religions have claimed to be concerned not just
with human attitudes and activities but with some reality or

realities to which those human attitudes and activities are a response. But the widespread incidence of religion throughout human history cannot by itself validate the truth of even the most basic beliefs implicit in religious experience and practice. Other beliefs—in witchcraft or the flatness of the earth—have been virtually universally held at one stage of the world's history; we do not for that reason hold them to be true today. There is no conclusive answer to those who regard religious belief as similarly illusory and in the early stages of disappearing from the category of seriously held human beliefs. No more can the intensity with which a religious belief is held authenticate the reality of that other in which a person believes. It is not uncommon to find that beliefs which are held with the utmost conviction turn out in fact to be false. Moreover it is difficult to dispute that there is an interpretative element in religious belief and a convinced believer may be entirely sincere in his beliefs and yet mistaken in the interpretation he gives of their cognitive character. Thus neither the widespread nature of religion nor the intensity with which religious beliefs are held gets rid of the problem of the elusiveness of the theological subject-matter with which we began. Indeed the very varied nature of religions and of religious beliefs is a part of the problem. Nevertheless the strength of the phenomenon of religion within human history is not without significance. The theologian is not being unreasonable in treating an area of human experience as widespread and as persistent as religious experience, as something to be taken very seriously; something that may contain within itself highly significant pointers to the true nature of the world and of man's place in it.

How then can a general study of religion proceed? In what is generally called the phenomenology of religion the question of the reality of any objective correlate of man's religious response is set on one side, and the attempt is made to describe as clearly as possible the nature of religion as experienced and as practised. The enterprise is beset with serious difficulties. One such difficulty is the definition of what is to count as a religion. I have already suggested that Marxism, for example, is in some respects very like a religion;

in other respects it is clearly very unlike. But even if the problem of definition is, at least for practical purposes, overcome, any such treatment is bound to be extremely formal and abstract. Religion as such is an abstract concept. People have religious experiences within the context of particular religions. These may have common features. Most religions have at least a ritual, a social, an ethical and a doctrinal dimension. But these take very different forms and are related to one another in very different ways. If we are to move beyond a very generalized level of treatment, our study will have to take the form not just of a study of religion but a study of religions.

If religion is worthy of study, then particular religions must be worthy of study; and if particular religions, then Christianity. Just as in the study of history there is a case for concentrating attention on the history of one's own country rather than studying world history in an inevitably superficial way, provided it is done with a proper recognition of the world context within which it is set, so there is a natural and justifiable case in a country with a Christian tradition for the special study of Christianity, provided it is not done in an insular and exclusive way. As long as such study remains at a phenomenological level, the parallel is apt enough. But the study of religion cannot be kept wholly at that level. No religion is content to be so treated. For virtually all religions, as I have already insisted, speak first and foremost of some supra-human reality addressing man or pervading the world in which man lives. They cannot even be understood in a serious way unless the question of the truth of their claims about that something other to which each religion is a response is taken seriously. Thus a study of Christianity inevitably gives rise to a study of Christian theology. And at that point there is a clear difference between the religious case and my historical parallel.

Does this mean that Christian theology ought only to exist as a subsection within the Comparative Study of Religions? The difficulties in that conception are both theoretical and practical. The presence of the word 'comparative' in the traditional title tends to suggest the existence of a neutral standpoint from which all religions can be surveyed and compared. But I have already argued in relation to the parallel case of agnosticism and faith that no such neutral standpoint exists. It is possible, as was also suggested in that earlier discussion, for someone to have sufficient empathy to enter into some genuine measure of understanding of a faith to which he does not actually subscribe. Thus Muslims have been heard to say that they have found their own faith enlightened and deepened by the writings of the Christian author, Kenneth Cragg. Such achievement is rare indeed. Yet it is only when something of that sort has been done, when someone has entered at the level of real understanding into two different religious faiths, that any genuinely comparative study can begin. It is a process which cannot be hurried, and certainly requires as its first stage a deep knowledge of particular religions.

The vital question for the would-be Christian theologian is how much does he need to know of other religions in order to ensure that his study of Christian theology will not be narrow and exclusive. No straightforward answer can be given to that question. He needs to have enough knowledge to ensure that he has a positive attitude towards religions other than his own. Only so is he likely to avoid the danger of speaking in his Christian theology of a tribal god of the Christians when he should be speaking of the God who is Lord of all the earth.

The exact relation between Christian theology and religious studies depends partly upon how the two titles themselves are understood. The phenomenological study of religion is of great importance to the theologian, because the category of religious experience is one of vital significance for theology today. And the study of other religious traditions provides a context which may help him to see the Christian faith in a truer perspective and save him from the temptation to make unwarrantably absolute claims for his own theological affirmations. But provided Christian theology pays serious attention to such studies—as it must also do to other studies of a non-religious kind—it remains a sufficiently substantial and coherent subject of study in its own right.

II

Christian Theology from the Inside

I. BIBLICAL STUDIES

Study of the Bible, I have argued, is not co-extensive with
the study of Christian theology. But it is a fundamental part
of it. The study of any book requires some degree of sympathy
with its subject-matter if one is to get beyond a superficial
level of interpretation. A measure of religious insight is therefore important for the interpretation of religious literature
and history. But religious books from the past are not only
religious, they are books. They are literature and history;
and whatever else may be appropriate to their special function as religious writings, there are no grounds for exempting
them from the kind of critical study that is used in the cases
of other literary and historical writings from the past. Let us
therefore begin there.

It is not my aim to give a detailed account of how critical
study of the Bible is carried on in contemporary theology.
My aim will be simply to indicate the kind of work that is
done and its place in theology as a whole. And I propose to
begin by considering six common-sense questions which arise
naturally in relation to any ancient text.

(i) *The language*
The Bible is available to us in a variety of English versions.
But none of it was originally written in English. The original
language of the Old Testament (with the exception of some
Aramaic chapters in Daniel and Ezra) is Hebrew, and of the
New Testament, Greek. The serious biblical scholar will
need to know Hebrew and Greek so that he can read his
texts in their original languages. For something is always lost

truth. So they 'corrected' their text to read what they believed it must originally have said. One example will suffice to illustrate the type of problem involved.

The New English Bible gives two translations of Gal. 2:3–5, one in the main text, and one in the notes at the bottom of the page. They read respectively:

Yet even my companion Titus, Greek though he is, was not compelled to be circumcised. That course was urged only as a concession to certain sham-Christians, interlopers who had stolen in to spy upon the liberty we enjoy in the fellowship of Christ Jesus. These men wanted to bring us into bondage, but not for one moment did I yield to their dictation; I was determined that the full truth of the Gospel should be maintained for you.

Yet even my companion Titus, Greek though he is, was under no absolute compulsion to be circumcised, but for the sake of certain sham-Christians, interlopers who had stolen in to spy upon the liberty we enjoy in the fellowship of Christ Jesus, with the intention of bringing us into bondage, I yielded to their demand for the moment, to ensure that gospel truth should not be prevented from reaching you.

They correspond to two different manuscript readings, which differ only in that one has and one has not got the Greek word for 'not' at the beginning of verse 5. Now it is theoretically possible that that little two-letter word was added or omitted by sheer inadvertence. But it is much more likely that it was added or omitted deliberately. In the second century there were some Christians whose understanding of Paul was such that they could not conceive for a moment that he would ever have consented to Titus's circumcision; but there were other Christians who could not conceive that there was ever such a division between Paul and the leaders of the Jerusalem church as Paul's refusal to have Titus circumcised would imply. Each group accuses the other of having tampered with the text at this point. One of the accusations is probably true, but it is not easy to be sure which.

So the biblical scholar, using essentially the same methods as those of the classical scholar, has to try to determine what the original text was. Sometimes the varied pieces of evidence all point in the same direction and he can set out the conclusion of his detective work with confidence. At other times the evidence will seem to point in differing directions and he must remain uncertain. In general the biblical scholar is well served by his texts. While many points of detail have to be left undecided, uncertainty about the true text seldom affects issues of major importance for the understanding of the biblical writings.

(iii) *The occasion of writing*

Many of the biblical writings are anonymous. Some of those which do claim to be the work of some particular author were not in fact written by the person whose authorship they claim. Few writings tell us the specific time or occasion of their writing. Yet knowledge of the author and of the situation for which his work was written may make a substantial difference to the way in which that work is understood. The biblical scholar has therefore to ask whether there is internal or external evidence enabling him to determine the authorship and date of the various writings he studies.

Two examples from the Old Testament will serve to show how basic such questions are. The first five books of the Bible, known as the Pentateuch, were believed according to Jewish tradition to be the work of Moses. That view was taken over by the Church and received general acceptance there; indeed in the Authorized Version they are subtitled the five books of Moses. It was sometimes allowed that detailed points might properly be ascribed to a later hand; not surprisingly, for example, the account of the death of Moses in Deuteronomy 34 was usually (though not always) allowed to be a later addition. But it was only in the seventeenth century that the claim to Mosaic authorship came under general challenge and little more than a hundred years since the main lines of the critical analysis of sources were established by two German scholars in what has come to be known after them as the 'Graf-Wellhausen' theory. Critical problems continue to abound and much further important work goes on, but we can now say with confidence that the various law codes embodied in Exodus, Leviticus,

Numbers, and Deuteronomy were not in fact laid down by Moses before the entry of the children of Israel into the promised land in the way the text describes. It is only when we have come to recognize that these law books as we now have them are the product of a much later age than that of Moses that the subsequent history of Israel and the teaching of the early prophets make any sense at all.

Similarly the book of Daniel appears on the surface to be a work written at the time of the Israelites' Babylonian exile in the sixth century B.C. Yet, as was pointed out by the anti-Christian Neoplatonist philosopher, Porphyry, in the third century A.D., its primary historical allusions are to a later date and particularly to the time of Antiochus Epiphanes in the second century B.C. If the traditional early date is maintained, the book will be taken to incorporate a remarkable amount of detailed predictive prophecy about the movement of world empires in the three centuries after it was written. If on the other hand we treat it, with virtually all modern scholars, as a work of the second century B.C. which uses ancient stories about Daniel for its own purposes in the crisis of the Jewish persecution at the time when it was written, then both its immediate intention and its broader religious significance are seen in a totally different light.

The same type of question is fundamental to the study of the New Testament also. Its importance there is perhaps less immediately obvious and its solution often more difficult to determine, but it is every bit as crucial. Who were the evangelists? What was their relation to Jesus? When and with what purpose in view did they compose their gospels? One cannot undertake to interpret the gospels without first making a serious attempt to answer those questions.

(iv) *Sources*

Writers do not write only about things they have experienced at first hand. Historians in particular have to rely upon the testimony of others when they write about the past. In assessing any historical writing we have to ask about the sources that were available to the historian and the use he has made of them.

The most obvious distinction between different types of source that an author may have used is that between written and oral sources. There are some cases within the Bible where we can be virtually certain that the author made use of at least one written source because we have that source in the form of another scriptural writing. Thus it is evident that the author of Chronicles knew and made use of the books of Kings. Similarly very few scholars would dispute the view that the author of Matthew's gospel knew and made use of the gospel of Mark. No doubt there are other cases where the author has drawn upon an earlier written source; but where that source has not itself survived it is not easy to be sure. There is value in tracking down such written sources, though their importance can easily be exaggerated. They push back the evidence for the events described a stage nearer in time to the events themselves, but questions have still to be asked about the reliability of the source; nearness in time does not in itself prove reliability of substance. The value is greatly enhanced where the source itself is also extant. By seeing what the author has omitted from his source and how he has modified its account of events, we can learn a great deal about what was important to him and about what he was aiming to achieve by his work.

But oral traditions can be just as valuable as written ones. When divergent strands of tradition were first identified in the books of the Pentateuch, there was a tendency to think of each distinguishable source as having been embodied in a document. Today more scholars are likely to speak of them as differing strands of oral tradition. Oral tradition in such cases is not simply a matter of transmission by word of mouth from one individual to another. It is more often a matter of folk tales or community traditions that had an important rôle in the continuing life of the community as a whole. To see the sources of the Pentateuch in that kind of way is not so much to take them out of the realm of serious historical knowledge as to show the long-standing importance of the stories involved for the religious life of the people.

Similarly, in the case of the first three gospels, usually

known as the synoptic gospels, scholars stress the way in which many of the stories of Jesus' ministry have probably taken their present form as units of preaching or oral instruction in the life of the Christian community. If these stories have been modified for the purposes of preaching or instruction, their value as precise evidence for the life of Jesus itself is certainly reduced, though it is not entirely destroyed. But there is gain as well as apparent loss in the process. For the close relation of the story to the actual life of the Church may help us to see better what its religious significance was for those who first told it and heard it.

(v) *Intention*

With the aid of these preliminary enquiries, one is in a position to ask the larger question: what was the author's intention and meaning in the work that he has written? We may understand the surface meaning of the words well enough but fail to grasp the author's real intention. All writings need to be interpreted against the background of their own age. There is always a range of unexpressed assumptions that are a part of the culture of the age, which are naturally shared by the author and his first readers but which may be completely overlooked by readers of a different culture or a different age. To interpret writings from the past we need more than a knowledge of the language and of the main historical happenings of the time. We need to know as much as we can of the general assumptions and expectations of the age, as well as of the particular character and concerns of the author. When an ancient writer speaks of the miraculous or of the demonic, we need to know the general attitude of people of his day to such concepts if we are to understand what he is saying. If we impose our own attitudes, as men of a scientific age, upon the text we shall fail to read his meaning correctly. It may well be that we cannot see or understand things entirely as he did, that his ways will always remain in some degree alien and opaque to us. But some measure of understanding of the ideas of the past is possible and that measure can be increased by an imaginative study of the records and the culture of a past age. It is perhaps the most difficult and the most important aspect of the historian's craft.

(vi) *Reliability*

Traditionally the question people have most readily asked of the Bible is: is it true? It should already be clear, and will I hope become clearer as this study proceeds, that that question is not as straightforward as it sounds. But there are certainly specific points within the biblical records about which it can be asked in a comparatively straightforward way. The Bible contains historical affirmations of a factual kind whose accuracy needs to be tested. This can be done in various ways. There may be other evidence relating to the same event within the Bible itself; some of the incidents in the life of Paul that are recounted in the Acts of the Apostles are also referred to by Paul himself in his letters in a way that puts a rather different construction upon them. Again, there may be appropriate external evidence either in the form of inscriptions—one in Delphi, for example, tells us that the Gallio of Acts 18:12–15 'who cared for none of these things' became proconsul of Achaia (the exact title Luke uses of him) in July A.D. 51—or of other documents—the Jewish historian Josephus, for example, gives his own independent account of such incidents as the execution of John the Baptist and the sudden death of Herod Agrippa I, which Luke records in Acts 12:19–23. And where such other evidence is non-existent or inconclusive we have to make judgements on the basis of the plausibility of the account as it stands. But even when dealing with issues of this more straightforward kind, caution is needed.

The question must always be asked within the context of the author's aim and the expectations of the age. What looks to us like a simple historical statement may have been intended by the author and understood by the original readers in a purely symbolic sense. When Mark spoke of a rending of the veil at the death of Jesus, it sounds like the account of a specific historical occurrence. It may be that Mark so understood it, though certainly seeing in it also a symbolic meaning of the opening up through the death of

Jesus of a way of access into the holy of holies, the presence of God himself. But it may be that he intended it in a purely symbolic way, and that in asking whether it actually happened as he describes it we are failing to grasp his real intention.

The question of factual accuracy needs to be asked not only in relation to specific historical occurrences, but more generally in relation to the balance and fairness of the scriptural records as a whole. The accounts which the various writers give are, like all accounts, selective in what they see as important and in the way they present the events which they record. Are their accounts sometimes misleading simply because of the inevitably limited standpoint from which they are written? And are there occasions where a more explicit bias has led to gross misrepresentation of the true picture? How fair, for example, is St. Matthew's account of the Pharisees or St. John's depiction of the Jews?

The kind of answer I have so far given to my sixth question about the truth or reliability of the biblical text will appear very inadequate to any one approaching it with a more general concern about the truth of the biblical message in mind—and rightly so. For the answer touches only the periphery of such an enquirer's concerns. In the questions I have been asking so far and in the way I have dealt with them I have confined myself to issues that could be raised about any ancient text and to the kind of treatment they might receive from the most detached of ancient historians. Those questions should be asked in that sort of way of every text, but they are not the only sort of questions that can properly be asked. With a play of Sophocles or a dialogue of Plato, for example, we may want to go on and ask about their meaning and their truth for us today. What is involved in pursuing these further questions?

Clearly the question of understanding must come before the question of truth. You cannot assess the truth of a Platonic dialogue without first understanding the argument. The first question to be answered then is the meaning of the text. This question is closely related to but not identical with the question we have already asked about the intention of the author. The meaning of a text is not simply to be equated with the author's intention. There may be meanings of which he was not consciously aware. In the case of a novel or a drama we may properly speak of meanings that arise from the interaction of the text with the minds of later readers or audiences. Moreover in view of the cultural differences to which we have already referred it may be impossible for the original meaning to become in its original form the personal meaning for the later reader. None of these possibilities does away with the importance of the historical questions concerning the intention of the author. That cannot be bypassed. Even though it cannot be decisive for all the various shades of meaning, it is normally an important constituent in determining them and a valuable check on interpretations of a purely arbitrary or subjective character.

Let us take as an example St. Mark's presentation of Jesus as the apocalyptic Son of Man and the conqueror of Satan. There is, as we have recognized, a difficult historical task to be done in determining just how Mark understood and intended these ideas. Whatever conclusion we may tentatively reach on the subject (and it is bound to remain tentative), it is almost certain that it will involve ways of understanding the world that are alien to our own contemporary ways of thought, beliefs about the world that we do not and cannot share. But we can nonetheless gain some approximate idea of what they meant for Mark. Can we go on and say what they mean for us? At one very literal level of interpretation we may be inclined to say that as we cannot share Mark's meaning his words cannot have a contemporary meaning for us. But that is not the only answer that can reasonably be given. Mark's account, we may say, depicts Jesus as a final embodiment of God's age-long purpose for mankind and as one who provides for man new possibilities for the overcoming of evil. Some such statement, it might be claimed, expresses the meaning of Mark's text for us in a way that no account in terms of his own beliefs about an apocalyptic figure or a conqueror of the demons could do. A prominent example of interpretation of this kind was the 'programme of demythologization' outlined by the German scholar, Rudolf Bultmann, in a famous essay in 1941, which became a central issue of theological debate in the years following the Second World War.[1] What he set out to do was to interpret what he called the mythological concepts of the New Testament in terms of a contemporary existentialist philosophy.

Any such approach to the text is clearly open to serious challenge. Is it a genuine form of interpretation at all? When does it cease to be interpretation and become rather an alteration or reduction of the original into something different but more acceptable to the interpreter? The difficulties and the dangers admittedly are great. But they are difficulties shared by every interpreter of the thought of an alien culture, for even the process of understanding another culture in its own terms at any depth involves some imaginative grasp of what would be roughly equivalent in the interpreter's own culture and experience. Nor need the difficulties be regarded as insuperable, if we recognize that what we said earlier about the impossibility of providing exact equivalents when simply translating from one language to another is bound to apply here even more strongly.

The dangers are greatly enhanced if the theologian makes the assumption that every passage of scripture must have a meaning which is not only intelligible to him as a modern man but also fully acceptable to him as true. When this assumption is made the likelihood of forced interpretations becomes very great. But as long as he is approaching the Bible in the way in which he would approach any other text from the ancient world, the critical scholar is not justified in making any such assumption. For the moment our concern is simply with the question of meaning, and we have argued that it is both possible and legitimate to go beyond the meaning of the text for the original author and his contemporaries and to ask what it conveys to us in terms of our own understanding of the world. Indeed the attempt to do so is already implicit in any attempt to grasp the author's own meaning. Not all texts, inside and outside the Bible, lend themselves

[1] R. Bultmann, 'New Testament and Mythology', in ed. H. W. Bartsch. *Kerygma and Myth* (London, 1953), pp. 1–44.

very fruitfully to questions of that kind; but some texts, both inside and outside the Bible, do.

Only when we have asked our questions about the author's intention, about the reliability of his information and the fairness of his attitudes, and about the meaning of the text for us ourselves are we in a position to raise the even more fundamental question about the truth of what is being said. Even if we have understood Mark's presentation of Jesus in a way that could make sense in the contemporary world, we have still to ask whether Mark was right. Is it true that Jesus is the final embodiment of God's age-long purpose for mankind and one who provides for man new possibilities for the overcoming of evil? Some views of the Bible as revelation would claim that that question answers itself, that if that is what St. Mark's gospel is saying, it must be true. We shall be considering such claims very shortly. But if the question cannot be given any pre-emptive answer of that kind, it raises issues outside the sphere of the literary and historical critic of the Bible. He can supply some of the relevant evidence, but the answering of the question will have to involve the doctrinal scholar and the philosopher as well.

These then are the sorts of question that the biblical scholar puts to his text. There are no rules of thumb by which one can learn to answer them and be sure that one is answering them right. There is evidence to go on but the evidence has to be weighed and different people of equal skill and ability will draw differing conclusions from it. One of the factors that tends to affect the scholar's judgement is the presuppositions with which he approaches his text in the first instance. This can affect even the earlier stages, such as the determination of the true text. I suggested that some of the errors that have come into the text, such as the different versions of the account of Paul and the circumcision of Titus, have got there as a result of theological bias. Bias of the same kind may also affect the scholar's judgement of what represents the original reading. A passionate upholder of justification by faith alone is likely to feel that there is more to be said for the reading that shows Titus as not being circumcised than for the other. And in relation to some of the later questions in the series I have outlined, the influence of the scholar's presuppositions is likely to be even more far-reaching. What judgement, for example, is to be given about the general character of St. Mark's gospel as a historical record? Ever since the priority of Mark as the earliest of the three synoptic gospels was established in the first half of the nineteenth century, this has been an issue of particular concern. We can see something of the ways in which Matthew and Luke used their sources, because we can see how they have modified Mark's gospel which they had before them. But what sources did Mark have and how freely did he adapt them for his purposes? Here there is little firm evidence to go on and it is not easy for the scholar to detach his judgement on the historical question from his general conviction about how important it is for Christian faith that there should be a basically reliable historical account of the life and ministry of Jesus. Those for whom that is a matter of great importance are inclined to give a more conservative account of Mark's intentions and achievements as a historian than those for whom the inner character of faith is less linked to historical fact.[1] We cannot escape from such presuppositions, but we can be aware of them and make some allowance for them. The work of biblical scholarship can be carried on in a way that leads to responsible judgements, which can be subjected to rational argument and counter-argument, even though it cannot be carried on in a way that leads to assured conclusions on all issues of major importance.

I began by saying that the Bible, being a religious book from the past, was not exempt from the kind of critical enquiry that scholarly study would employ in relation to any other book from the past. But what implications does the Bible's special rôle as Christian Scripture have for the theologian's study of it? Traditionally in Christian faith the Bible is seen not simply as one religious book among others, but as uniquely authoritative, embodying the unique revelation of God. It is for that reason that it has been valued and

---

[1] Cf. pp. 103–4 below.

given its special place in the life of the Church down the ages. What is meant by such claims for the Bible? Do they affect the way in which it ought to be studied? I wish to consider three ways in which the claim that the Bible is uniquely revelatory has been understood.

(i) *Revelation in words*

The Bible is a book or collection of books. If then it is said to be God's uniquely authoritative word to men, it is not unnatural to understand such a claim as implying that all the statements of the Bible are true statements, guaranteed free from error and conveying divine truth to man. At times this has been understood in an extreme form which postulated that God dictated the words and that the rôle of the human author was a purely passive one. Thus Athenagoras in the second century A.D. spoke of the Old Testament prophets as a flute played upon by God the flute-player, and Gregory the Great in the sixth century spoke of the scriptural writers in general as of no more significance in the writing of Scripture than the pen in the hand of the author— in this case the Holy Spirit. Clearly a position of that kind would render most of the types of enquiry I have just been describing irrelevant. If the Bible is so unlike any other book in the manner of its composition there is no point in submitting it to the same type of investigation that one would use in the case of other books.

But the position has not often been held in quite such an extreme form as that. Gregory had argued that since the human author was no more than the pen in the hand of the true, divine author, it was sheer waste of time to concern oneself with questions about his human situation or psychology. But the third century writer, Origen, the first great biblical commentator, took a different view. He shared with Gregory the belief that the true meaning of Scripture, once discovered, was God's meaning and wholly trustworthy, but God had hidden his treasure in earthen vessels. The differing human authors had left the stamp of their different styles and personalities upon the text. John is described in Acts 4:13 as 'illiterate' and the fact that he actually followed his father

into the poor profession of a fisherman was for Origen further
testimony of a background with little education. The marks
of his shortcomings were evident in the style of his gospel and
the interpreter needed to make allowances for that fact.
Similarly Paul describes himself in 2 Cor. 11:6 as 'unskilled
in the use of words' and the interpreter who has struggled
with the more involved of his sentences may feel that there
was truth in his self-depreciation. But all such modification of
the position affected only the outward form. The inner meaning was still God's meaning, still 'true' without qualification.

Now it is quite clear that at the factual level any such
claim is false. One has only to compare, for example, the
conflicting accounts of the same historical incident in different books—or even variant traditions within the same
work. Did David pay fifty shekels of silver or six hundred
shekels of gold for the site of the temple (2 Sam. 24 and
1 Chr. 21:25)? Did David kill Goliath or did Elhanan (1
Sam. 17 and 2 Sam. 21:19)? In such cases, and there are
many of them, the accounts cannot both be factually correct.
In themselves the points at issue are trivial enough, but they
constitute evidence which makes it impossible today to maintain with any degree of plausibility at all the claim that the
Bible is free from error of any kind. The claim is likely therefore to be still further modified and to take the form of a
claim that the Bible is free from doctrinal error or from error
in those truths that concern man's salvation. This is a much
more elusive claim, since it is not immediately clear what are
the truths that concern man's salvation. Certainly there are
within the pages of the Bible very varied accounts of the
nature of God and of man's destiny. Some of these accounts
are of a kind that would be repudiated by most Christians
today. Was it God's command that Joshua was fulfilling
when he had Achan and all his family stoned for purloining
some of the spoils of Jericho (Joshua 7:10–26) and that
Samuel was obeying when he 'hewed Agag in pieces before
the Lord' (1 Sam. 15:33)? Even in this form, then, the claim
that the Bible is uniquely revelatory in the sense that it contains the truths that concern man's salvation in a form that is
wholly free from error is remarkably difficult to sustain. The

very varied character of the biblical affirmations themselves
cries out against any such assessment of its status.

If positions of this kind are as difficult to sustain as I am
claiming, it may seem surprising that they are still held as
widely as they are. The reason, I believe, is that it has seemed
to many people that only if something of this kind be true can
Scripture be understood as revelatory in any serious sense.
They feel that they have to choose between holding that the
Bible is free from error on the one hand and ceasing to treat
it as a religiously authoritative book at all on the other. It is
therefore worth pointing to other arguments against any
claim to inerrancy on behalf of the Bible in addition to the
empirical evidence of the actual character of the biblical
writings themselves. We ought not to regard a revelation in
words free from error as the theoretically ideal form of revelation though one which we have regrettably to acknowledge
to be unrealized in practice. Such a revelation would fit very
ill with the kind of God-given world in which man finds
himself. Nowhere in our general experience of the world do
we find any comparable approach to certainty in matters of
personal or religious significance. Any such account of revelation would turn it into something almost totally discontinu-
ous in kind with our ordinary experience. It would involve
enormous difficulties in the understanding of God that it
would imply and would make any attempt to give a coherent
account of our experience as a whole virtually impossible to
achieve. These arguments do not claim to be conclusive.
They do not render it logically impossible for revelation to
have taken the form of an inerrant biblical text. But they
have, I think, sufficient force to suggest that when we come
to consider other ways in which the revelatory character of
Scripture has been understood, we do not need to approach
them as if they were religiously inferior to the kind of account
we have been considering so far. They may well emerge not
only as more consonant with the evidence, but as religiously
more appropriate as well.

(ii) *Revelation in events*
We speak of the Bible as the Word of God. But it has also

been spoken of as the book of the Acts of God. The distinction between the two is not an absolute one, because we know of the acts primarily because they are recorded in words. But to lay the stress of God's revelation on the events which the Bible records certainly corresponds to one very important strand of thought within the Bible itself.

The decalogue is a portion of Scripture which has probably been treated more readily than any other as something that can be lifted out of its immediate context and regarded as the timeless revelation of God's will for man. Yet in their initial appearance in the book of Exodus, the ten commandments are set out as the response called for by the prior saving act of God in rescuing his people from Egypt. 'I am the Lord your God who brought you out of the land of Egypt, out of the house of bondage. You shall have no other gods before me . . .' (Exod. 20:24). So time and again in the Psalms, in the writings of the prophets and in the New Testament, there is a pointing back to past saving acts of God as the place where his power and his grace have been made known. The revelatory character of the Bible on this account lies in the witness that it bears to these great events, which are the true locus of God's self-revelation.

This location of God's revelation in the events which the Bible records rather than in the words of the Bible as such avoids some of the difficulties that render the other account untenable, but it has serious difficulties of its own to face. We will look briefly at three of these.

I have already indicated that the distinction between words and acts cannot be rigorously drawn. Events cannot be separated from the way they are understood. The mere fact of the escape of the children of Israel from Egypt, however miraculous its attendant circumstances, would not have been revelatory unless it had been understood as God's redeeming act and as establishing a covenant relationship between him and the people of Israel. Any understanding of revelation has therefore to be linked not simply with the happening as such but also with a particular way of interpreting it.

It is not easy to say what it is that constitutes certain

events as revelatory acts of God. It is sometimes suggested
that it is the miraculous character of such events as the
crossing of the Red Sea, the Virgin birth, or the resurrection
that shows them to be special acts of God. But the miraculous
nature of the event is neither a necessary nor a sufficient
criterion in the eyes of the biblical writers themselves. Nor
does a simple distinction between acts recorded in the Bible
and those not so recorded seem a satisfactory criterion. The
events of which the Old Testament speaks are too much part
and parcel of the general history of the ancient Near
East.

Nor indeed does it seem possible for a theologian today to
regard all those events which the Bible itself sees as revelatory
acts of God as all being such in the same sense. Can the
drowning of the Egyptians in the Red Sea be equally revelatory of the same God as the crucifixion of Jesus?

(iii) *Revelation in Christ*

Considerations of this kind have led most of those who want
to stress that the revelation of God is embodied in the events
which the Bible records to draw distinctions between the
events concerned. They are not to be seen simply as an
arithmetical series in which each one is of exactly equal
significance. Rather they constitute a pattern. The Epistle to
the Hebrews begins by contrasting the way God had spoken
in fragmentary and varied fashion through the prophets in
the past with his full and final address to mankind in the
person of his Son. The essential location of God's revelatory
words and acts is the person of Christ. Other events have
their lesser revelatory character by virtue of their relationship to him. The authority of the Bible is derivative from the
authority of Christ and is constituted by the Bible's witness
to him.

Such an account has an immediate and proper religious
appeal for the Christian because of the central rôle which it
ascribes to the person of Christ. But what is meant by speaking of revelation as essentially located in Christ? Much of the
New Testament is concerned with the life and thought of the
early Church after the life of Jesus on earth was over. It is to

that period that the most profound and far-reaching accounts of who he was and of the meaning of his life, death, and resurrection belong. Indeed the nature of our records is such that it is very difficult for us to separate out what really derives from Jesus himself and what derives from the varied responses of the early Church to him. So the Christ whom we know from the pages of the New Testament is a composite whole —Jesus as apprehended by the early Christian communities. The early response to Jesus cannot therefore be excluded from this central locus of revelation.

Where then are we to stop? The Old Testament, which on this theory is revelatory because of its preparatory rôle in relation to the coming of Christ, goes right back to Adam. Why should not the response be carried on equally far in the other direction? Traditional Roman Catholic teaching has affirmed that 'revelation constituting the object of Catholic faith was completed with the apostles' (Lamentabili, 1907). But it is difficult to see how any firm distinction of that kind can be drawn between the later writings of the New Testament and the roughly contemporary writings of the earliest of the Apostolic Fathers. We have to acknowledge that there is a certain arbitrariness about the precise limits of the canon, about what finally was included and what excluded from the contents of the Bible.

There is no doubt that this third approach is an improvement on the other two as an attempt to state why the Bible should be seen by the Christian as embodying a revelation of God. But it too has its difficulties when we try to understand just what is involved in the notion. Certainly the closeness of its witness to Jesus is a primary reason for the particular importance that the theologian attaches to the Bible. Yet we have to acknowledge that on that score alone there are sources, such as the Dead Sea Scrolls, which are of as much importance as some parts of the Old Testament and that there is no essential difference in kind between some of the New Testament writings and the subsequent records of Church history. The Bible as embodying the writings which the Church selected as its central witness to Christ rightly demands the special attention of the theologian. But that does not mean that it calls for any special method of treatment that would not also be applicable to other records that have to do with the coming of Christ and men's response to him in the life of the Church. The theologian may rightly give more time and attention to the attempt to grasp the meaning of the biblical texts for himself than he does to other texts from the later history of the Church, but in doing so he will, as we have seen, be doing something that he can, and at times will, also undertake in relation to other texts as well. The revelatory character of the Bible does not make its call on his attention exclusive of all other calls. The subsequent history of the Church is not just an addendum to the study of theology proper. It is an integral part of it.

2. CHURCH HISTORY

I have argued that there is no pure knowledge of Christ accessible to us which can be separated out from the forms of human response to him, and that for that reason the history of such responses is an integral part of theological study. Ideally this would include all aspects of the history of the Church. But if the study of church history is not to be hopelessly superficial, some specialization is inevitable. Traditionally, the greatest stress has been placed on the early history of the Church. There is a strong case for this. Sometimes the claim is made that the developments of the Church's life, and particularly its doctrinal decisions, during that early period before the great divisions within the Church had arisen have a special authority for the Church today, second only to that of the Bible. But whatever our judgement on that issue may be, the outstanding importance of the period for the whole subsequent life of the Church is beyond dispute. For it saw a development of the Church's beliefs, its organization and its worship into comparatively fixed forms which are still extremely influential today. It also saw the transformation of the Church's position in society from that of a persecuted minority to that of being the officially favoured religion of the Roman empire. It is from that early period that I shall take my illustrations in this discussion of church history. But the same principles apply and could just as well be exemplified from other later periods.

The historian needs to develop an attitude of suspicion and distrust. He must not accept the evidence of his sources at their face value without first submitting them to critical scrutiny. Most of the documents available to him were written not to provide the future historian with a balanced selection of evidence but to make out a particular case. Even if there is little or no evidence favouring the opposing position, this may well be because only evidence favourable to the party that actually triumphed has been allowed to survive. The evidence that is available to us may mislead either because we lack the background knowledge against which to interpret it correctly or because it was deliberately fabricated to give a false picture which the author wished to persuade his contemporaries to accept as true. Documentary evidence, which is the historian's primary source material, is particularly liable to mislead in this way. It needs to be supplemented by other kinds of evidence, such as that provided by archaeology. But stones need to be interpreted as well as books. They too can mislead. I want to illustrate the kind of detective work that such historical work involves and to show its fundamental importance for our understanding of the past with the help of three examples from the time of the early Church.

Documents may belong to a quite different period from that to which they claim to belong. There is an important corpus of theological writing claiming to be the work of Dionysius the Areopagite, mentioned in Acts 17:34 as one of the few who responded positively to the preaching of Paul at Athens. The writings give expression to a highly systematized trinitarian theology, drawing extensively upon the neoplatonic ideas of the later Hellenistic world. They are the work of a man, whose name is unknown to us, writing about 500 A.D. The fifth and sixth centuries were a time when the Church was particularly suspicious of novelty. It stressed the nature of Christian faith as something 'once for all delivered to the saints'. Tradition was the primary criterion of truth. So our writer wished to present his ideas as embodying the truth of the gospel from its earliest days. Until about the sixteenth century his writings were accepted as coming from the end of the first century. To accept them as very early works is not merely to see them in a false context; it leads to a totally distorted picture of the development of early Christian thought. For it means that those who struggled their way through the third and fourth centuries to a fully-fledged trinitarian belief were not after all pioneers feeling their way forward for the first time into the true implications for man's understanding of God of Christ's coming into the world. That had been accomplished by Dionysius in one fell swoop two centuries before. Their debates would have to be seen as a curious kind of shadow boxing with the real creative insights already achieved elsewhere. Dionysius is by no means the only example of such pseudonymous writing in the life of the early Church. Unless such pseudonyms are recognized and the writings ascribed to their real situation, no authentic understanding of the Church's history is possible.

But documents may also be deliberately altered or added to at a later date. The historian's task would be easier if his documents were seamless wholes, belonging, for example, either entirely to the first century, or entirely to the fifth. For then one decisive piece of evidence could locate the whole document in its true setting. But that is not always the case. An instructive example is the important correspondence of Ignatius, martyr bishop of Antioch, early in the second century. Eusebius, the fourth century church historian, speaks of seven Ignatian letters. The Middle Ages knew various versions of the Ignatian correspondence, some including as many as thirteen letters. Since the letters speak in high terms of episcopacy, there was a strong tendency in the sixteenth and seventeenth centuries for Catholics to defend the genuineness of the letters and for Protestants who had rejected the episcopal form of church government to deny it. It was not hard to find evidence pointing in either direction. But scholarly work, by Archbishop James Ussher (better known as the man responsible for calculating the date of the creation of the world as 4004 B.C.), was able to show that seven of the letters (with certain additions expunged) were genuine writings of Ignatius and that the others belonged to a later date. The crucial evidence was the form in which Ignatius was quoted by other writers in the intervening years before the expanded version was devised. Important confirmation of this detective work was forthcoming shortly afterward; only two years after the publication of Ussher's work in 1644, an early Greek manuscript was discovered closely agreeing with the hypothetically reconstructed version of the genuine letters.

Furthermore most documents have a specific bias of which account needs to be taken. Many writings of the early Church period are concerned with heretical teaching. Their aim is not to give a carefully balanced account of the heretic's position. It is rather to use every available means to ensure that this false teaching will not lead believers astray to the detriment of their eternal salvation. And every available means frequently included misrepresentation both of fact and character. One comparatively trivial example will suffice to illustrate this principle of far-reaching importance. I take it from Eusebius the church historian, for the writing of church history itself has frequently been concerned not merely to present a chronicle of the past but rather to show how the story of the past indicates a particular theological position. In his account of Paul of Samosata, who was condemned for heresy by a local council at Antioch in 268 A.D., Eusebius reports Paul's accusers as saying that 'he put a stop to psalms addressed to our Lord Jesus Christ, on the ground that they are modern and the compositions of modern men, but trains women to sing psalms to himself in the middle of the Church on the great day of the Pascha, which would make one shudder to hear'. It sounds unlikely behaviour on the part of one, who even if found guilty of heresy, was at the time bishop of Antioch. If it were true in the sense that Paul's accusers (and probably Eusebius himself too) would like us to accept it, we would surely have a case not so much of a heretical bishop as of an anti-Christian egomaniac. Now Paul was undoubtedly a powerful personality, perhaps somewhat vain and egotistical. He would not be the last bishop in

Christian history of whom that was true. His particular 'heresy' involved a strong insistence on the unity of God and a reluctance to see Christ or the Son as a distinct person of the Godhead. Prayer in the early Church, as witnessed by the prayers embodied in St. Paul's letters, was normally offered to God through Christ, as is still characteristic of the formal liturgical worship of the Church today. It would not be unnatural for Paul to regard the practice beginning to develop about that time of offering worship in the form of hymns addressed directly to Christ as a regrettable innovation and for him to use his authority against it. Whether he were right or wrong to do so, there was a serious theological case to be made out for his position. It was easy and attractive enough for an opponent to present his action as one more evidence of his evil vanity. But to treat such accounts at their face value leads to a grossly misleading picture of the Church and the issues with which it had to deal.

The fundamental approach of the church historian to his sources that I have been describing is very similar to that of the biblical scholar outlined in the previous section. There is nothing surprising in that, for it is essentially a method of historical criticism which the biblical scholar employs. But it helps to reinforce the propriety of seeing the Bible as continuous with the ensuing records of church history, if we recognize that precisely the same types of problem that I have used to illustrate the methods of the early Church historian occur also in the New Testament. 2 Peter is almost certainly a pseudonymous work to be dated in the second century and not a letter written by the apostle himself. The Pastoral epistles may well incorporate some genuine Pauline letters, worked over and considerably enlarged by someone a generation later. And the Paul who could say of his Judaising opponents, who were insisting on the necessity of circumcision, 'as for these agitators, they had better go the whole way and make eunuchs of themselves' (Gal. 5:11), can hardly be trusted to give a scrupulously fair account of their position or their motives.

The primary concern of the Christian theologian is with what is to be believed about God in the light of the event of

Christ's life, death, and resurrection. In his study of the history of the Church he will therefore give special attention to the way in which the Church has formulated its fundamental beliefs down the ages. As a historian he will insist that any such formulations cannot be studied in isolation from their immediate historical circumstances, but any formularies solemnly accepted by the Church as a whole call for particularly careful study. The Apostles', Nicene and Athanasian creeds are described by Article VIII of the Church of England as creeds which 'ought thoroughly to be received and believed' and they command a very wide measure of acceptance among most Christian bodies today.

The historian, as we have seen, will not be so trustful as to take them at the face value of their traditional descriptions. He will not be surprised to discover that the Apostles' creed was certainly not composed by the Apostles and, though something like it can be traced back to the second century, derives in the form that we now know it from seventh century France. The so-called Nicene creed is not the formulary agreed upon at the famous ecumenical Council of Nicaea in 325 A.D. but comes from the Council of Constantinople later in the century. The so-called Athanasian creed was certainly not by Athanasius (it was originally written in Latin, not in Greek), nor indeed is it strictly speaking a creed. It probably derives again from France in the fifth century and was designed for teaching purposes.

But the historian's chief concern will not be with the occasion of their writing. That is a necessary preliminary to the main task of understanding their contents. When the Nicene creed speaks of the Son as 'of one substance with the Father' (let alone the more detailed trinitarian affirmations of the Athanasian creed), it is not saying something that is self-evidently true about God in the light of the scriptural witness to Christ. How did such affirmations come to be made? What lies behind them? And what was intended by them?

One line of answer would suggest that from the beginning the Church had a clear and definite gospel to proclaim. This the heretics tried to contradict or to confuse, usually from reprehensible motives. The work of the Church Fathers, which finds formal expression in the creeds, would then be seen as a restatement of the original gospel in more precise terms in a way that would effectively exclude the errors introduced by the heretics. But it does not require much historical study to show that this kind of account will not do.

In the first place the Christian gospel was less unified at the outset than such an account suggests. But more importantly the process of transition from earlier forms of belief into the more detailed ideas of later Christian doctrine was of a far more problematical character. In very general terms the issue may be seen as one of translation from primarily Jewish to primarily Greek categories of thought. The conception of God that was most characteristic of Hellenistic thought in the early centuries of the Christian era and that had the greatest attraction for Christian thinkers was one that derived primarily from Platonic tradition. The perfection of God was thought to consist in his absolute changelessness, his impassibility, his pure and undifferentiated unity. But those Christians who instinctively shared much of this lofty monotheistic outlook believed also in a gospel which spoke of God the Father and of God the Son, a gospel whose glory was God's costly involvement with the affairs of men. It was not easy to combine such a conception of God with such a gospel. But that was what the Fathers, partly consciously partly unconsciously, set out to do. There was a determined attempt to hold on both to the underlying philosophical convictions and to the experiences of which the gospel spoke. It was as part of such an undertaking that the creeds were hammered out. It was a situation in which there were no obviously right answers. If the creeds are to be treated seriously and not as mere shibboleths which testify to party loyalty, they have to be understood in terms of that particular historical setting. It is an important part of the church historian's task to elucidate the nature of such developments in Christian thought.

It is also important that church history should not be isolated from the history of the world outside. This principle is already implicit in what has just been said about the need to interpret the history of Christian doctrine in terms of the general intellectual and cultural ideas of the age. But the interrelation of the history of the Church and of the world applies not simply to the history of ideas. It operates at many different levels. Two examples will suffice.

The history of the Church in North Africa in the fourth century is very largely the story of conflict between the Catholic Church and a powerful schismatic movement of a puritan kind, known as Donatism. Now there were explicit points of theological dispute between Catholics and Donatists, such as the attitude of the Church to Christians who had lapsed under persecution and whether or not those who had been baptized by some schismatic body ought to be re-baptized when admitted to the main body of the Church. These differences were real and sincerely held. But the division between Catholic and Donatist was not exclusively theological in origin. Local feeling against Rome, economic grievances of the poor against the rich, opposition of peasants against city-dwellers—all these had some part to play in the Donatist protest. It is part of the task of the church historian to try to clarify and to assess the rôle of these various factors in the story.

When Athanasius wrote the life of Antony, the first Christian hermit, he depicted him as departing to the desert as the result of a personal response to the challenge of Jesus to the rich young ruler recorded by St. Matthew, 'If you would be perfect, go, sell what you possess . . .' (Matt. 19:21) as he heard it read in church. But it is clear that the rise of monasticism had other causes as well as response to the world-denying challenge of the message of Jesus. The Egyptian desert had seen ascetics before the Christians made their way there. When Basil, the first great monastic organizer, writes about Christian asceticism, he draws extensively on pre-Christian Greek ideals of detachment from the affairs of the world. The change in the position of the Church from that of a persecuted minority to that of a group specially favoured by the emperor, the general unsettlement in the social and political life of the empire as a whole and the heavy burden of taxation borne by the middle classes at the time, all played their part. Once again it is the rôle of the historian to trace the interaction of such very varied factors—cultural, political, and economic. Religious and theological factors were and are important in their own right, but they never function in isolation. To ignore their interrelation with social and political factors is to fail to see things as they really are.

In these varied ways the Church historian seeks to understand how and why Christians have come to believe and to act as they have. But there is a further question, which cannot properly be asked apart from such understanding but which the historian himself cannot answer. Are those beliefs true?

3. CHRISTIAN DOCTRINE

To move on to this further question is to move into a more precarious area of study where the appropriate method to follow is more difficult to determine. It certainly cannot be undertaken at all without the aid of the kind of critical study of the Bible and of church history that I have been outlining. But can it be undertaken even with their aid? In the past it has commonly been asserted that at this point theology becomes inescapably confessional. The decision as to what forms of Christian belief are true was thought to be a matter determined simply by confessional loyalty and not by the kind of open and critical discussion that operates in, for example, the historical field. Today many more theologians would want to undertake the study of Christian doctrine with an openness of approach much more closely akin to that which is characteristic of biblical and historical study.

The changing attitudes to this part of theological study over the last hundred years can be well illustrated from the history of the Oxford school of theology. When that school began just over a hundred years ago it was still possible to speak of Oxford as in a real sense a 'Church university'. Until 1871 subscription to the Thirty-nine Articles was required of every member of the university. At that time the study of Dogmatic Theology was simply a study of the early creeds, since they were held to embody the true beliefs of the Christian Church and of the Church of England in particular. In 1904, in line with the changing status of the university, the content of the examination was changed to 'the History of Christian Doctrine to 461 A.D.'. I have already argued that a historical study of that kind is an essential preliminary to any proper study of the creeds. But as a course of study in its own right it remains simply at the level of history. Today every student has to do a paper not only in the history of Christian doctrine to 461 A.D. but also in 'the Christian Doctrines of God, Human Nature, and Salvation'. The current assumption therefore is that Christian doctrine itself, as well as the history of doctrine, can be studied in the open and critical way that is characteristic of the modern university.

But can this in fact be done? Can a religious man live by his faith and at the same time submit the substance of that faith to a properly rigorous and critical scrutiny? There are various ways in which the attempt has been made to show how Christian doctrine can both provide that assurance which is necessary to the life of faith and also be subjected to honest and unprejudiced enquiry. We will look at two main lines along which this has been attempted.

The first approach distinguishes between an essential, inner core and its broader intellectual elaboration. A distinction of this kind is implicit in the traditional attitude to the creeds as embodying the essentials of Christian belief. It is most explicitly developed in the Roman Catholic distinction between dogma and theology. Every subject of study, it may be claimed, is based on certain underlying axioms. Theology is no exception. The axioms with which the theologian works are expressed in the form of certain dogmas. These are revealed truths, explicitly and officially declared by the Church to be such. In those cases, the truth of what is affirmed is guaranteed by the Holy Spirit. Theology, by contrast, is the attempt to elucidate those truths and to apprehend their significance more fully. All such theology is tentative, open to continuous criticism and revision.

The inherent weakness of such a position will be evident from our earlier discussions. It does not seem possible in practice to fence off an area of dogmatic affirmations of that kind and ascribe to it an unqualified certainty. Dogmatic utterances and credal statements are too firmly embedded in their various historical contexts to be separable from them in the way that such a theory demands. Certainly there are affirmations from the past that are of central importance to the theologian, but we are not justified in treating them as unquestionable axioms.

For reasons of this kind the distinction is sometimes put in a different way which is not so vulnerable to such criticism. The distinction may be made in terms of a contrast between inner essence on the one hand and any verbal formulation of it on the other. In words from Pope John XXIII's inaugural address to the second Vatican Council 'the substance of the ancient doctrine, contained in the deposit of faith is one thing; its formulation is quite another'. This certainly avoids the basic difficulty of the other theory. Dogmas and creeds are not now being treated as absolute and unquestionable. They are not to be identified with the inner essence; they are particular formulations of it. The difficulty in this case is the elusiveness of the concept of 'inner essence'. Christianity down the ages has shown itself a very varied phenomenon in its ethos as well as in its intellectual formulations. Is there an 'inner essence' of the faith that was common to a Greek monk on Mt. Athos, a devout Italian peasant of the fourteenth century and an equally devout Wee Free highlander of the nineteenth? It may be that there is, but can the doctrinal theologian know whether or not he is being faithful to it in the doctrinal judgements that he makes? The distinction is one of importance; but it does not by itself clarify the task of the doctrinal theologian very much.

The other approach sees objectivity of theological study as something guaranteed by its character as response to the Word of God. This way is characteristic of Reformed theology and is particularly associated in recent times with the name of Karl Barth. God, it is insisted, is not properly to be spoken of as the object of theological study. God's relation to man is always that of personal subject. It is he who in his sovereign freedom addresses man. And in doing so he imposes the appropriate form in which he is to be understood upon those who listen with responsive and obedient attention to

that address embodied in the Word of God. Analogies may
be drawn with such diverse forms of study as physics and art.
In physics, it is claimed, the world of objects outside us
imposes itself upon us and demands to be understood in
particular ways appropriate to its nature. This may involve
fundamental and very difficult changes in human conceptu-
ality as some of the developments in physics in the twentieth
century clearly testify. The study of art would appear to be a
far cry from the study of physics. But Professor Torrance,
who has made a great deal of the analogy between modern
physics and theological science, has also described Barth as
having 'the eye of the artist who has the faculty of seeing
what is actually there and can pick out its deepest and most
characteristic forms with which to depict and to communicate
it so that his own creative art is allowed to be the instrument
of the reality of his subject'. To the unartistic, the work of the
artist may seem to be a wholly subjective activity, in the
sense that 'every man does that which is good in his own
eyes'. But most artists would claim that, though what they
are doing is something intuitive and non-deductive, it is
nonetheless not arbitrary but a genuine interpretation of
reality. So it is claimed with our knowledge of God. It cannot
be deduced by rational argument. But the reality of God and
the appropriate form of theological speech about him are not
arbitrary. They are objectively given where there is the
appropriate kind of attentive listening.

There are aspects of this approach that are of great importance for the theologian and I shall try to develop some of
them later. But as a general defence of the objectivity of
doctrinal study, it claims too much. It does not do sufficient
justice to the importance of changing historical conditions.
Its shortcoming in this respect can be illustrated from the
character of Barth's own theological work. The central
emphasis in his writing, that which imposed itself upon him
as fundamental as he attended and responded to the Word of
God, was that God cannot be known by human reasoning,
but only as he chooses to reveal himself to men. A Lutheran
critic, Gustaf Wingren, has commented that in his view this
is not so central a theme in Scripture as justification by faith.

Barth, he claimed, had been strongly influenced by the particular needs of his age. He was aware of that sense of the
absence of God that grew up in the post-enlightenment era
and found therefore in the Word of God the message of
divine self-revelation which was particularly apposite to the
needs of the time. Sensitive attention is undoubtedly essential
to theological work. But the appropriate forms of theological
speech are not given to us from outside with the degree of
objectivity that Barth suggests. We contribute a good deal
more from the particular experiences of our own times and
our own situation to the substance of theological belief. This
inescapable element of subjectivity must be fully acknowledged in any account of doctrinal method.

Both these approaches that I have outlined are rightly concerned to find an objective core to theology, which will not
be open to the charge of being purely arbitrary and subjective. They seek to present the subject as one which is open to
rational discussion while at the same time having the firmness
which religious faith seems to demand. One seeks it in a
dogmatic inner essence, the other in a given form of theological speech intuited through obedient attention. Both
seem to me to be too inclined to seek for their anchor of
objectivity in one particular, isolated element within theology. I want to suggest that no such element can be isolated,
but that the method by which the doctrinal theologian works
does nonetheless have the quality of rational discussion about
it which is appropriate to its subject-matter. I propose to set
out this method in terms of a coalescence of the basic characteristics of the two greatest theologians of the century, Karl
Barth and Paul Tillich.

Barth defined dogmatic theology as 'the scientific test to
which the Christian Church puts herself regarding the
language about God which is peculiar to her'.[1] In other words
it was an activity carried on within the Church in an attempt
to test the truth and the adequacy of the language used in
the worship of the Church and the proclamation of the
gospel. Tillich, on the other hand, described his theology as

[1] K. Barth, *Church Dogmatics* (Edinburgh, 1936), Vol. 1, pt. 1, p. 1.

an 'answering theology', one which set itself consciously to answer the questions posed by the non-Christian world of his day. Neither in practice was exclusive of the approach stressed by the other. Barth, as we have seen, could not, had he wanted to, have prevented the questions of the co ntemporary world affecting the nature of his critical reflections upon the Church's traditional language. Tillich was emphatic that one could only answer the world's question out of the store of Christian tradition from the past.

How then can these two approaches be combined into a responsible doctrinal method? A great deal of theological study is a form of dialogue with the past. Biblical study and church history are our attempt to gain an accurate and sympathetic understanding of the Christian past. The doctrinal theologian then relates to the understanding he has gained from these studies the questions which are being posed by his own age, by both Christians and non-Christians. By reflection upon the correlation of these two concerns, he seeks to be able to answer the question: what then should Christians say today?

There is no rule of thumb method by which that question can be answered. But there is no rule of thumb method for making historical or literary critical judgements. The judgements that the theologian makes will not be unrelated to the faith by which he lives. But they will not be wholly determined by it. The evidence with which he wrestles will have repercussions on the precise form that his faith will take. If they are judgements of faith, they are certainly not judgements of faith in the sense that they are arbitrary and incorrigible by reasoned argument. They are judgements of faith in a sense which has close analogies with other forms of study. There is a particularly instructive analogy with the work of ethics.

A good deal of the work of the student of ethics takes the form of a dialogue with the past. He will not be taken very seriously as a student of ethics unless he has wrestled with the work of Plato and of Aristotle, of Bentham and of Hobbes. An important part of his study will be historical in character. But however important that historical study he will not simply take over and commend as they stand the theories of past writers. He will pay attention to the problems of the present, the ethical issues with which men are being faced and the ways in which they deal with them both theoretically and practically. Can he then go on to say: these things then are good, while those things are evil?

At that point there is a considerable division of emphasis between different scholars. Nowell-Smith, at the end of his book on Ethics, shows himself very reluctant to do so. He sees the work of the moral philosopher as essentially descriptive and believes that the genuinely moral judgements have to be left to each individual on his own:

Moral philosophy is a practical science; its aim is to answer questions in the form 'What shall I do?'. But no general answer can be given to this type of question. The most a moral philosopher can do is to paint a picture of various types of life in the manner of Plato and ask which type of life you really want to lead. . . . The questions 'What shall I do?' and 'What moral principles should I adopt?' must be answered by each man for himself; that at least is part of the connotation of the word 'moral'.[1]

Iris Murdoch, on the other hand, is critical of those who seek 'to "neutralize" moral philosophy, to produce a philosophical discussion of morality which does not take sides'.

Moral philosophy cannot avoid taking sides, and would be neutral philosophers merely take sides surreptitiously . . . Since an ethical system cannot but commend an ideal, it should commend a worthy ideal. Ethics should not be merely an analysis of ordinary mediocre conduct, it should be a hypothesis about good conduct and how this can be achieved. How can we make ourselves better? is a question moral philosophers should attempt to answer.[2]

Murdoch's position seems to me to be the more satisfactory of the two. At one level, certainly, a man's moral decisions and his religious beliefs must be his own. But that does not

---

[1] P. H. Nowell-Smith, *Ethics* (London, 1954), pp. 319–20.
[2] Iris Murdoch, *The Sovereignty of Good over Other Concepts* (Cambridge, 1967), pp. 1–2.

mean that the moral philosopher or the theologian has to limit himself to a description of the past and then leave the matter entirely to the individual. There is a creative rôle by virtue of which they can guide men by setting out the reasons how and why they should judge or believe in certain ways. They can provide a framework of morality or doctrine within which the individual will be able to make a more informed and responsible decision. The criteria of judgement in both cases are enormously difficult. There is no simple procedure for determining what is right in either case. But there is the possibility of an intelligible method of discourse in which evidence can be weighed and the relative strengths of different possibilities rationally assessed. No comparable branch of study can ask for or lay claim to more than that.

4. PHILOSOPHY OF RELIGION

In the first part of the introduction, I stressed the elusive nature of the subject-matter of theology. The theologian, it was argued, has no way of guaranteeing the reality of his basic subject-matter, namely God himself. He has no way of proving that his subject is not in the end as unreal a discipline as astrology. Yet the subsequent discussion of biblical and historical studies has taken no obvious cognizance of this fact. It has proceeded as if there were no special oddity about the subject-matter of theology. That indeed is how theology itself proceeds for most of the time. It cannot continually be contemplating the problematical character of its fundamental categories. It must get on with its own job, working with its appropriate categories, problematical or not. That is a perfectly proper procedure, provided the theologian is not thereby led to believe that that underlying problem has ceased to exist or to be of any importance. The fact that biblical study can be carried on in a coherent and developed way, all the time taking the assumption of God's existence entirely for granted, is no guarantee that there is after all such a reality. Nor does the Bible itself deal very directly with this question. The first commandment is not that men should acknowledge God in some way; no such commandment was needed. It is that he should acknowledge only one God. Even the fool of whom the Psalmist speaks who says in his heart that there is no God is not an atheist or even an agnostic in the modern sense. His denial of God is spelt out more fully later in the psalm as a denial that God will call him to account (Ps. 10:4, 13).

Yet the reality of God or the gods has not always been taken for granted in the way that it was in the days of the Psalmist. Historically the need has been felt for rational support for belief in the existence of God. Today it is certainly vital that theology should concern itself with the possibility of such reasoning. Part of the rôle of the philosophy of religion is to ensure that the theologian is kept constantly aware of this problem and the nature of the issue that it raises. I want to begin by considering how far the philosophy of religion can make a constructive contribution to this particular and fundamental problem and then go on to discuss the more general critical function of the philosophy of religion in relation to theology as a whole and to theological language in particular.

The great theologians of the scholastic period, such as St. Thomas Aquinas, sought to maintain the general position that man's unaided reason was able to provide a firm substructure for Christian belief, though revelation was essential in order to build fully upon it. Reason, for example, could demonstrate *that* God is, the bare fact of his existence, but revelation was necessary to show *what* God is, that, for example, he is a trinitarian God, three persons in one substance. Traditionally three main arguments have been appealed to as proofs of God's existence. They are usually known as the ontological, the cosmological, and the teleological arguments or, to translate their names into less technical language, the arguments from being, from the world and from design.

The ontological argument is the most difficult of the three to grasp on first hearing and certainly the one that carries least immediate conviction for most people. The argument begins by defining God as 'that than which nothing greater can be conceived'. It then asks us to imagine two people holding the same conception of God, but one of them denying his existence while the other affirms it. The only difference between their two conceptions of God is that the former's lacks existence while the latter's has it. Surely, so the argument goes, the conception of God as existing is the greater of the two. But since God is by definition 'that than which nothing greater can be conceived', only the second is truly a conception of God at all. The claim that God does not exist turns out to be self-contradictory, because one can always conceive something greater—namely that same God actually existing. So God's existence is proved simply by reflection on the meaning of the word itself. Thus the ontological argument claims to achieve its goal without even having to refer to the existence of the world.

The cosmological argument, by contrast, finds its starting point in the existence of the world, in the fact that things exist at all. Everything, it is then argued, can be traced back to a prior cause. The idea of an infinite regress of causes is claimed to be absurd, and we are forced therefore to postulate the idea of a first cause. This first cause must be different in kind from everything else, being self-explanatory in a way that the existence of the world is not. It must exist necessarily and not just contingently. This necessary being, which is the first cause of all other existents, is what we mean by God.

Finally, the teleological argument begins one stage further on. Its starting-point is not *that* the world is, not the mere fact of the world's existence, but rather *how* the world is, the general character of the world we do in fact know. That general character, it is argued, is not random, it shows order or design. The way in which the world is adapted to meet the needs of organic life, particularly human life, is far too complex to be the outcome of sheer chance. So extensive and intricate are the signs of ordered purpose in the world at large that they can only be construed as evidence of a creative designer of the whole, in other words, of God himself.

Part of the task of the philosophy of religion is to assess the very varied ways in which these and other cognate arguments have been developed. The one thing that would be almost universally agreed is that, whatever force they may have, they are certainly not valid as deductive arguments. We cannot go into the details of the counter-arguments any more than we have been able to do for the arguments themselves, but the reasons for denying them the force of deductive arguments are not hard to see. In the case of the ontological argument the primary objection is the logical fallacy involved in treating 'existence' as if it were just one more predicate that might or might not apply to things in the same way that other predicates do. In the case of the cosmological argument, it is not self-evident that the category of cause is of such universal application. It can be regarded simply as a way of understanding the relation of one thing within the universe to another. The validity of speaking of a first cause or of a cause of the universe as a whole can then be called in question. Many of the examples of order in nature of which the teleological argument speaks look rather different in a post-Darwinian age, though knowledge of evolution does not undermine the argument entirely. Even more damaging is the greatest of all difficulties for theistic belief, the problem of evil. If the elements of design that we can trace in nature are evidence of God as designer, they are not on the face of it very good evidence for the existence of the beneficent and omnipotent God of Christian theism.

The significance of these debates for our immediate purpose is their confirmation of the fact that there is no firm escape from what I have called the problematical character of theology's fundamental subject-matter, namely God himself. In the case of certain kinds of logical or mathematical argument, one may reach a point at which, if someone has apparently followed the argument but refuses to accept the conclusion, one has good ground for dismissing one's interlocutor as someone who simply does not understand what reasoning is. But whatever may be said about the rational justification for theistic belief, it is emphatically not of that kind. We have therefore to go on and ask whether if we cannot have incontrovertible arguments for the existence of God, we can perhaps have arguments of a somewhat different kind. But before doing so, we need to ask whether arguments of any kind are in fact necessary at all. I have already indicated my own conviction that they are, but I want to look in a little more detail at the position of those who claim that one is better off without them altogether.

Nowhere is that attitude more trenchantly expressed than in the famous words of Pascal that were found after his death sewn into the lining of his coat.

Nov. 23, 1654. FIRE. God of Abraham, God of Isaac, God of Jacob, not of the philosophers and scientists. Certainty, certainty, feeling, joy, peace. Forgetfulness of the world and of all except God. He is to be found only by ways taught in the gospel.

Many others before and after him have felt deeply that same contrast between the God of Abraham and the god of the philosophers. Whatever philosophical argument may be able to do, one thing they have felt certain it was unable to do and that was to point to the living God of Christian faith. If the objection is simply that such arguments are not sufficient to elicit faith in God as the practising Christian knows it, the point may readily be granted. It has never been claimed that they were. Such reasoning has always gone hand in hand with an appeal to revelation of some kind, though the relationship between the two has been understood in a wide variety of ways. But to say that a line of argument is not sufficient does not rule out the possibility that it may still be necessary.

But the objection may also be raised in a stronger form which challenges not only the sufficiency of philosophical reasoning for establishing belief in God but its propriety in any form at all. Such reasoning is sometimes presented as in direct conflict with the way of faith, as a refusal to recognize the prior nature of God's initiative in reaching out to man. When God speaks to man, the only appropriate response is that of the child Samuel in the temple, 'Speak, Lord, for thy servant heareth.' (1 Sam. 3:9). To look for proofs of God's existence, to ask as it were for God's credentials, is to succumb to the basic sin of human pride.

We have already seen something of this approach in the course of our discussion of doctrine. This insistence on the absolute necessity of attentive obedience has an impressive

note of religious seriousness about it. It needs for that reason
to be taken seriously and to be treated with respect. Nevertheless the theologian has, I believe, to insist firmly in reply
that in the form here put forward it will not do.

It is true that psychologically reason plays a comparatively
small part in determining most Christians' initial adherence
to that faith. The same is true of most people's adoption of a
moral attitude or of a political standpoint. In all such cases
reasoning more often takes place from within an already
adopted position, testing and justifying its validity. Such
testing is no mere shadow boxing. People do change in their
religious, moral, and political allegiance, and reasoning often
has a part to play in bringing about such changes. Unless we
ascribe some rôle to reason and to argument, then quite
literally there would be no reason for holding the Christian
faith rather than the faith of a black-power Muslim or a Nazi
in the days of Hitler's Germany. For many of the adherents
of those movements, their faith is apprehended as an external
address demanding a response of absolute obedience with the
same kind of direct self-authenticating character which the
Christian opponent of the rôle of philosophical reason
describes.

Philosophical reasoning in defence of one's religious faith
may also be rejected for philosophical rather than directly
religious reasons. Some philosophers, following up hints contained in Wittgenstein's talk about different 'language-
games' and distinct 'forms of life', have drawn the conclusion
that no intellectual communication on the issue is possible
between believer and unbeliever. The religious man has his
reasons but they only have meaning within the context of
the particular way of life practised by believers. But such a
rigorous separation between the patterns of thought and
speech within the believing community and that outside does
not seem to correspond to the facts of the case. The languages
and the lives of believer and unbeliever are far more inter-
woven with one another than that. Communication between
them may often be blurred and imperfect, but it does exist.
There does not appear to be any adequate philosophical
ground for denying altogether the possibility of the believer's

reasons being sufficiently intelligible to the unbeliever for rational discussion between them to take place.

If then some form of reasoning in relation to the question of belief in God is desirable and at the same time is not to be ruled out as impossible, what form can it take? Since it cannot as we have seen be of a strictly deductive form, the most natural suggestion to make is that any argument should take the form of a probability argument. It may not be possible to prove that God exists, but it may be possible to show that it is more probable that he does than that he does not exist. But caution is needed in putting the case in this way. Probability in the stricter sense of the word is still a mathematical notion. Our normal way of making probability judgements is on the basis of comparison with other comparable situations. If we say that it will probably rain tomorrow, we do so (if we are speaking carefully and not expressing a general pessimism) because on the majority of past occasions when the weather conditions have been similar to what they are now, there has been rain on the succeeding day. But in reasoning about the existence of God we are unable to argue in that way. We cannot say that all the universes we have met in the past which were as ordered as this one were the work of a divine creator and that the same is therefore probably true in this case also. There is only one universe and there are therefore no comparable situations on which a probability judgement can be based.

But reasoning does not have to be either of a deductive or strict probability kind. In the moral and aesthetic spheres, for example, it may follow a looser and more intuitive form without ceasing to be reasoning. It is to reasoning of this broader kind that we need to look.

If stress is laid on the intuitive character of this broader kind of reasoning, it may be spoken of as a form of apprehension rather than of argumentation at all. 'The starting point of natural theology', wrote Howard Root, 'is not argument but sharpened awareness.'[1] An analogy has sometimes been drawn with the seeing of a puzzle-picture in a new way. The

[1] H. E. Root, 'Beginning all over again' in ed. A. Vidler, *Soundings* (Cambridge, 1962), p. 19.

same picture can be seen, for example, as either a staircase or as an overhanging cornice. Seeing the picture in a second distinct way is not something to which a person can be brought by argument; he is convinced when he comes to see it in that way by a new form of awareness.

But it is important not to overstate the contrast between vision and argument, between sharpened awareness and reasoning. If reasoning is excluded altogether, we are back in the unsatisfactory position that I have just been criticizing of being unable to give any reasons for regarding the Christian vision as truer than any other form of awareness. Moreover it is not in fact correct to present vision and reasoning as mutually exclusive. Even in the visual example that I have been using, there are things that can be said which may help to give rise to the change of perspective involved in the revised way of seeing the picture. We can, for example, suggest that parts of the picture which the person at the moment sees as empty space be thought of as solid projections and vice versa. The importance of this kind of suggestion in giving rise to new forms of awareness becomes even more important when we move from the visual to the literary sphere. Two people may be disputing about the theme of a play that they have seen. They may initially have interpreted it in very different ways. Each will then try to convince the other by pointing to particular scenes or characters or sayings which are fully incorporated in and highly significant for his interpretation, but which are not effectively accounted for in the interpretation offered by the other. This is a form of reasoning, though if one is finally convinced by the other it will only be when, as we say, he comes to see the play in a new light. Reasoning and vision are integrally inter-related with one another.

Many other examples could be given from a wide range of everyday experience. For most reasoning is of this suggestive or cumulative kind. No individual argument is decisive; some evidence may always remain unexplained and may continue to provide the basis of counter-arguments whose rational character cannot be denied; but cumulatively a case is built up. The unique character of the subject-matter when such reasoning is applied to the existence of God, the lack of any strictly comparable situations, always remains a difficulty and makes such reasoning even more tentative than in other areas of debate. Nevertheless it does not rule it out altogether. The cosmological and teleological arguments are not valid deductive arguments. Nevertheless a sense of wonder at the existence of anything at all or at the emergence of consciousness out of the primaeval stuff of the universe is not a purely private experience felt only by religious believers. To call attention to it and to ask whether when proper attention is given to it it may not give rise to a vision of the world as dependent on a divine source and purpose is a proper form of reasoning. The claim of the theistic philosopher is that in the light of such features of our experience it is reasonable, even allowing for the counterweight of such other features as are embodied in the problem of evil, to affirm belief in the existence of God. He will not expect his reasoning to convince all other reasonable men, any more than the literary critic will expect everyone else to see a profound but difficult play in the way that he expounds it. The evidence is not of a kind that lends itself to demonstration of that sort. But nor is he simply talking to himself. He is making a contribution to rational discussion which is capable of being understood not only by those who agree with it but also by some at least of those who still remain unconvinced by it.

We began with an etymological definition of theology as reasoned discussion about God. So far we have been concerned with the problematical character of theology arising from the *theos* aspect of the word, from the fact that the reality of God is not something that can be proved or that it is absurd for anyone to deny. But there is a further and equally fundamental problem embodied in the *logos* aspect of the word, the question whether it is possible for us to speak rationally about God. This is something felt not only by the unbeliever who finds all talk of God unintelligible; it is felt also by the believer however convinced he may be of the reality of God's existence. Indeed very often the stronger his belief in God, the more problematical all talk about God may appear to him. For the more he is convinced of the

mysterious, infinite, and transcendent character of God, the
more likely he is to regard any words he uses about God as so
inadequate as to be worthless—or even blasphemous.

Some years ago I published a short article entitled 'The
Difficulties of being a Theologian'.[1] This provoked a spirited
retort from a mission priest in Korea, Roger Tennant,
entitled 'The Impossibility of being a Theologian'.[2] The
opening words of his article put the point so vigorously that
I quote them at some length:

'Theology is a distinctive activity within the pattern of Christian
life with its own peculiar methods and its own peculiar difficulties.'

'*To whom then will ye liken me, that I should be like him, says the Holy
One?* (Isa. 40.25). The answer is nothing; God is incomparable
and there is nothing with which we may rightly compare him.
And yet that is precisely what we have to do.'

'The Christian theologian has at least this measure of assistance
in his task, namely that he believes that God has revealed himself
to us in Jesus Christ. Here then is a further basic feature of the
Christian theologian's task, but it has its own inherent difficulty.'

These three quotations are from 'The Difficulties of Being a
Theologian', by the Rev. Maurice Wiles in *Theology*, May 1961,
p. 181ff. They produce in me a wild desire to laugh, to weep, to
blaspheme, a whole gamut of uncontrollable emotions going far
beyond the modest murmur of sympathy for the theologian's lot
that Mr Wiles is no doubt hoping to elicit. How to make these
chaotic emotions intelligible? If I fail in this task, at least let it be
recorded by the Angel that I made an inarticulate shriek of
protest.

'To whom then will ye liken me, that I should be like him says
the Holy One?' Could it be that the answer might be silence? No,
because as everyone knows, 'Theology is a distinctive activity
within the pattern of Christian life with its own peculiar methods
and its own peculiar difficulties'. There may be a few peculiar
difficulties, Lord, in likening thee to this or that; but do not
worry: we have our own peculiar methods. 'There is nothing

---

[1] *Theology*, LXIV, May 1961, pp. 181–4.
[2] Ibid., December 1961, pp. 503–5.

with which we may rightly compare him. And yet . . . that is precisely what we have to do'.

But why is it precisely what we have to do? What if it were precisely what we have *not* to do? What if the whole meaning of the Prophets, culminating in the coming of a man who is pictured as saying 'He who has seen me has seen the Father', were to prevent us from this vulgarity, this anti-poetry, this blasphemy, this sacrilegious hobby of 'theology'?

The difficulty is not a new one. Christians have felt it from the earliest times. Both their faith and their Greek sources spoke to them of the absolute distinction between God and man. Knowledge of God, said Clement of Alexandria, before the end of the second century, was strictly knowledge 'not of what he is but of what he is not'.[1] God is immortal, incorporeal, invisible: he cannot die, has no bodily existence, and cannot be seen. But all these characteristically negative words only tell us what is not true of God; they do not tell us positively what is true of him. This stress on the negative character of our knowledge of God has been an important strand in Christian theology throughout the history of the Church. It is known as the *via negativa*. Strictly God is ineffable; there is nothing that we can properly say about him. If that were the whole story, as some forms of mysticism would like to suggest that it is, the theologian would indeed be reduced to silence.

But men do in fact speak positively about God. A colleague on reading Mr. Tennant's article commented that, if I were asked to respond to it, he would recommend a four-word reply: 'Jesus called God "Father".' It may be a form of poetry, but are the poets to go uncriticized? Is one form of poetry as good as another? If we call God 'Father' are we not bound to give some sort of justification for our use of that name rather than some other? In practice the *via negativa* has seldom stood alone. Even those who have taken it most seriously have sought to combine it with another way, usually called the *via eminentiae*. Thus Clement of Alexandria, having stressed that our knowledge of God is only knowledge

[1] Clement, *Stromateis*, 5.71.

of what he is not, goes on a little later to give an account of
how we do use positive language about God in these terms:

Whether we use the name 'One', 'the good', 'mind', 'absolute
being', 'Father', 'God', 'creator' or 'Lord', it is not a question of
producing the actual name; in our impasse we avail ourselves of
certain good names so that the mind may have the support of
those names and not be led astray in other directions. For taken
individually none of these names is expressive of God, but taken
together they collectively point to the power of the Almighty.[1]

In other words the claim is being made that certain good
human characteristics can properly be used as indications of
the truth about God. Clement's language is cautious. He has
not forgotten what he has said earlier about the *via negativa*.
God is not simply the good things in human experience writ
large. But nevertheless the claim is there that human words
can be used, however indirectly, to indicate truth about God.
It is an important part of the philosophy of religion to consider what is involved in such a claim and how it can be
justified.

The traditional account that theologians have given of
their language about God has been to describe it as analogical. Analogy is in origin a mathematical term, implying
similarity between two things in some respects but not in
others. In particular it implies a similarity of structure or
pattern. When the concept is applied outside the mathematical field it is often used of things where the similarity is
hard to tie down, because there is a fundamental difference
of character between the two things being compared. Thus
we speak of a 'sweet taste' and also of a 'sweet sound'. Taste
and hearing are different senses and the word cannot therefore have precisely the same meaning in each case. Yet it is
the same word in each case—not a different word that happens to have the same spelling and pronunciation, as when the
thing one aims at in a game of bowls and the thing with which
one props up a car that has a puncture are both referred to
as a 'jack'. Knowing from firsthand experience what is meant
by both a sweet taste and a sweet sound, it is possible to see

[1] Ibid., 5.82.

what it is that makes the same word appropriate in both cases, though it is very difficult to express the connexion clearly in words. It is not so easy to be confident that anyone who had never heard the phrase, a sweet sound, would know at all accurately what it meant simply by analogy with the familiar concept of a sweet taste.

How then are words used analogically to refer to God? The word 'father' has a primary meaning; this is usually taken to involve a measure of love and care as well as the purely biological sense of male progenitor. It may then be used analogically at the human level. We may speak of the founder of a small business, who takes a personal interest in all those who work for him, as 'the father of the firm'. There is a similarity of structure between his relationship with the firm and all those involved in it and that of a father with his family, although the precise forms in which that relationship is expressed may be very different in the two cases. When the same term is further applied analogically to God, we are again saying that there is a similarity of structure between the situation where the word is used of human relationships and the relationship of God to the world.

The analogical character of language when referred to God does not apply only in the case of obviously metaphorical terms like 'father'. It applies also in the case of more metaphysical language. God is not wise in just the same way as men are wise, for human wisdom involves the concept of a good memory with recall appropriate to varied needs and a shrewd insight into complex situations. Such descriptions could not appropriately be used of the omniscient God. Nor does God exist in the same sense that all other things do. For all other existence is contingent, dependent on other things outside itself. If God's existence is necessary and dependent on nothing other than himself, it is something significantly different. Existence when referred to God does not mean just the same as it does when applied to anything else.

Such indirect use of language is obviously difficult to handle and easily open to abuse. When Augustine claimed that God was just but that his justice could not be equated with human justice, his claim was formally correct. But when he used that claim in defence of the justice of his extreme predestinarian views, it is natural to feel that the claim is being misused. One cannot but sympathize with the moral protest of J. S. Mill, when he declared: 'I will call no being good who is not what I mean when I apply that epithet to my fellow-creatures, and if such a being can sentence me to hell for not so calling him, to hell I will go.'[1] Yet while applauding the moral protest, one may still regard Mill's account of how words ought to be used as too oversimplified to be wholly satisfactory as an account of the use of language about God. All that his argument logically requires is a refusal to use the words 'just' or 'good' of God in senses that are in contradiction of or even that are substantially different from the senses they have when applied to human beings. It does not require that they should be used in the identical sense and therefore does not rule out absolutely the propriety of claiming that such language when applied to God ought to be understood analogically.

The scholastic doctrine of analogy was developed with far greater precision than the kind of account I have given might suggest. In my judgement it was in fact done with greater precision than the subject-matter itself justifies. Nevertheless something not altogether unlike it is inescapable if any account is to be given of how it is that we use language about God. Two of the ways which some recent writers have used may be mentioned.

Ian Ramsey, who was Bishop of Durham until his death in 1972, used to talk of models and qualifiers giving rise to cosmic disclosures.[2] The roots of his language lay in the use of models in scientific discourse, but he developed the idea specifically to give an account of religious language. A human concept such as fatherhood or goodness was for him a basic model. These are then qualified—almighty Father, infinite goodness—until a cosmic disclosure takes place, until, that is, a man comes to apprehend a mystery beyond words

---

[1] J. S. Mill, *Examination of Sir William Hamilton's Philosophy* (3rd ed. London, 1867), p. 124.

[2] See especially I. T. Ramsey, *Religious Language* (London, 1957), Chapter II.

to which he is brought by an infinite projection of the ordinary concepts of fatherhood or goodness.

Others, taking their start more from literary than scientific discourse, have described religious language as symbolic in character. A symbol is a concept or an object which embodies in itself a wide range of experience but also points beyond itself to depths beyond that which any individual has actually experienced. The origin of a symbol may be arbitrary (like a national flag); it may arise from particular historical occurrence (like the cross); it may be grounded in some universal experience (like light); or it may be a combination of historical and general experience (like Madonna and Child). But in every case it starts with some everyday concept or happening but extends it to convey some further and deeper range of meaning.

All these varied accounts of religious language have an imprecise and suggestive character about them. It is not surprising that their validity has been strongly challenged. Can anything so imprecise be more than an expression of human emotion? Has it any claim to be regarded as a form of reasoned discourse about God?

The challenge takes various forms. In its strongest form it has been held that propositions only have meaning if we can verify them (or at least know how we would verify them) as true or false by the difference they would make to our sense experience. In this extreme form the challenge would render meaningless vast tracts of our ordinary speech—most of our moral discourse for a start—and few would uphold it in that form today. But it is not unreasonable to claim that when we make an affirmation we ought to be able to state what counts as evidence for or against it. The claim for example that an invisible, intangible, and unsmellable elephant is sitting on this book as you read it is not false but nonsense, for nothing whatever is relevant to or involved in its truth or falsity. Some people would claim that statements about God fall into the same category. Does not the Christian claim that 'God is merciful' whatever states of affairs may come about for individuals or the world? But the Christian can reply that there is evidence (the life of Christ, for example) that is relevant to the description of God as merciful; there is also *prima facie* evidence that counts against it. The fact that there is no decisive way of settling the issue does not rule out the propriety of his making the affirmation. He can readily acknowledge that he can neither fully justify it nor fully understand it but that neither deprives it of meaning nor precludes him from continuing to affirm it. Despite the real difficulties inherent in speaking about God, it is not something that has to be ruled out altogether.

We began this discussion of our talk about God with the problems involved in applying individual words or concepts to God. In the course of it we have moved over into discussion about the making of affirmations about God. This is a natural progression, for the proposition affirmed is a more explicit container of meaning than the individual word or concept. But much of the talk about God in religious literature, and in the Bible in particular, comes in the form of stories. These stories are frequently spoken of as 'myths'. In what sense ought the theologian to understand the stories about God, which he seeks to use and to interpret, as mythological?

The word 'myth' is used in a wide variety of disciplines. It is basic to the work of the anthropologist, but figures prominently also in the study of literature, of psychology, and of political theory. Its proper definition is hotly debated. Its introduction into the work of theology in the nineteenth century was closely tied up with debates about the inerrancy and literal truth of the Bible. 'Myth' thus had a bad press in theology at the outset. To say that the story of the Garden of Eden was a myth was understood by the conservative majority to imply that it was not true; so to accept that parts of the Bible were mythical was, it was felt, to repudiate their truth and so to abandon them as divine Scripture. But myth is essentially a positive concept. It is an imaginative story, whereby a community expresses and so is better able to come to terms with some underlying truth or characteristic of its life. The story in question may be entirely fictitious, or it may be grounded in some specific historical occurrence. It may or may not involve the action of supernatural beings. In primitive societies it usually does. So does it also in those myths that are of special interest to the theologian. The story of Eve's seduction into sin by the serpent and the story of the fall of Lucifer are myths of this kind concerned with the origin of evil in the world. Old Testament myths like these have much in common with the myths that figure elsewhere in the literature of the Near Eastern world, and the work of the anthropologist can be of help towards their interpretation.

The language of such myths has obvious affinities with that of Christian theology as a whole. The fall story has become a basic element in the traditional Christian account of sin and salvation. Is the sending of God's son to redeem men from that sin equally mythical? The issue became one of prime importance for theology through the work of Rudolf Bultmann. For him the whole New Testament account of the coming of God's son into the world to do battle with Satan and the demons was understood as a myth, readily accepted in the first century but alien to the twentieth. If we today were to grasp its true meaning it needed, he argued, to be 'demythologized'. The truth that it conveys had to be freed from its mythological clothing. Only then would men of the twentieth century be in a position to see the real message of the gospel, and to respond to it whether positively or negatively for the right reasons.

The problem is a special case of the general difficulty of grasping the contemporary significance of a text from the past, which we have already raised in our discussion of biblical studies. Bultmann was clearly right in emphasizing the importance of recognizing the characteristic assumptions of the age in which the New Testament was written and the ways in which they differ from our own. It is more questionable whether it is possible to eliminate the mythological altogether from the language of Christian theology, as the word 'demythologizing' tends to suggest we should be seeking to do. The proper evaluation of myth as a vehicle of Christian belief continues to be an important issue in contemporary theology.

The Impact of Other Studies

In the eyes of some people science and religion are in direct conflict; others see them as utterly separate, having no contact with each other. In the face of such wildly differing judgements, we may reasonably expect to find that the real relationship between the two is a subtle and complex one.

It is important to begin with a historical review, however brief. For the theologian approaches his dialogue with the natural scientist with a guilty conscience. There are grounds for his doing so, but the actual grounds on which he does so are often wrong ones. The names of Galileo and of Darwin symbolize the theologian's unease about his predecessors' attitude to the work of the scientist, and I shall therefore confine my historical remarks to some general comments on the famous clashes in which they figured.

The Christian view of man sees him as God's vice-gerent in the universe. The incarnation underlines the centrality of man in the purposes of God, for there God himself is believed to have been actually embodied in the life of a man. If man is so central to the whole creative purpose of God, there would seem to be at the very least a symbolic appropriateness in the view that the earth is at the physical centre of the universe. Thus the natural implications of revelation supported the immediate evidence of the senses themselves that the sun moved round the earth. That conviction was part and parcel of a whole pattern of belief in which the senses, reason, and faith seemed harmoniously combined. Galileo's evidence was thus seen not as challenging one particular belief but a whole co-ordinated scheme of understanding.

Now clearly the centrality of man in the purposes of God and the physical centrality of the earth are not logically related to one another. But it was not unreasonable to see a profound significance in the presumed relationship between the two. So when the ecclesiastical opponents of Galileo set their faces against his new ideas they were not simply setting the *ipse dixit* of Scripture or of ecclesiastical authority over against the clear-cut evidence of scientific observation. They were not being as straightforwardly or simplistically obscurantist as that description would suggest.

Similar issues were operative in the Darwinian controversy. Undoubtedly a misguided belief in biblical literalism played an important rôle, but it was not the whole story. If man is made in the image of God, the concept of a special creation of man has again an obvious appropriateness. In this case also the link is not a logically necessary one but neither was it blindly unreasonable to affirm it. It seems to hold together in a satisfactory synthesis the empirical evidence of man's distinctiveness from the animals and the declarations of faith about his divine origin.

But however reasonable the basic attitudes of the resistant theologians may have been, they were unquestionably wrong. Their attractive synthesis did not conform to the facts of the case. I have stressed this particular aspect of the two stories (and it is only one aspect) because if we regard the theologians of the past in these disputes as simply guilty of invincible stupidity we shall not only be doing them an injustice, we shall also be less likely to appreciate their significance for any understanding of the relation between science and theology today.

In reaction to these disastrous debates of the past, there has been a tendency in the twentieth century to drive an absolute wedge between science and religion. The ways in which this radical separation is expressed vary. Science, it is sometimes said, deals with the objective world, with the world as it is, religion with the existential world, with the world as men experience it. Science deals with efficient causes, with 'how' questions, religion with final causes or 'why' questions. Science is concerned with empirical truth, religion with symbolic truth.

Now it is clear that science and religion are concerned with different questions. They do use different methods in their attempts to answer them. They do fulfil different rôles or functions. It is disastrous if these distinctions are not recognized and the two are simply confused with one another. Nevertheless it is the same world about which each asks and seeks to answer its different questions. And since it is the same world which each in its own way is seeking to interpret it would be surprising if whatever were discovered about the world by one was totally without bearing upon the work and findings of the other. The knowledge we have as a result of scientific research that the world did not come into existence suddenly at some moment in the past just in its present form but is the product of a gradual evolution affects the way we experience the world around us; it makes a difference therefore to the existential questions which the religious man today asks about the world. The two types of question cannot be kept in complete isolation from one another. There must be a relationship of some sort between them. How then is that relationship to be understood?

The problem is one that arises within science itself. Scientific explanation is not all of one kind. Events may be explained in terms of mathematical physics, or chemistry, or biology, or psychology, or sociology. These are different kinds of explanation, answering different questions and using different methods. Nevertheless they are not wholly distinct. There are connexions between them as well as discontinuity. We go wrong if we ignore or play down either the differences or the links between them.

The first error arises if we insist that what works well for one type of explanation must necessarily therefore be appropriate for another. Aristotle saw humans to be moved by the desire to fulfil certain goals in life. He used the same categories of explanation in the case of an animal in search of its prey and of a stone falling to the ground in search of its natural resting place in the centre of the earth. That did not prove a helpful way of explaining the fall of stones to the ground and we speak instead of a gravitational pull expressed in terms of mathematico-physical laws. But we would be making the same mistake if we argued from the greater fruitfulness of the mathematical physical explanation in the case of falling stones that ultimately a similar type of explanation ought to be provided for human and animal behaviour as well. What is fully appropriate to explain the movement of stones is not necessarily fully appropriate to explain the movements of men or of animals.

But there is a contrasting danger if we are tempted to look upon the different types of explanation as irrelevant to one another. The psychologist is right to insist on the use of his own categories and to resist any attempt to reduce them to the categories of chemistry or physics. But it is essential that he listens to and takes note of the biochemist's findings. For biochemical and psychological factors are inter-related in the life of man. A psychological depression may have an organic physical cause. But equally well a physical paralysis may be the result of some inner psychological trauma and be inexplicable in purely organic terms. There is a relationship between the two which must not be ignored even though it cannot be fully understood. It operates in both directions. The different descriptions cannot simply be combined into a single discipline but the frontiers between them are open and have continually to be redrawn.

Theology should be seen as having the same sort of relationship to the other sciences as they have to one another. The theologian is fully justified in operating with his own categories. He should resist the attempts of those who seek to eliminate them and confine him to the categories of ethics or psychology. But he cannot work with them without paying careful attention to the findings of the more precise sciences. The anti-Darwinians of the nineteenth century were not at fault in holding on to the category of divine creation. Their mistake was in their unreadiness to listen to what the scientist had to tell them about the nature of the created world and then to revise their own understanding of divine creation in the light of it. There may well be other cases today where the theologian still has similar lessons to learn. It may be that some traditional theological affirmations about miracle or providence or intercessory prayer are in conflict with what the scientist can show us about the way the world is. If so they must be revised in the light of his findings. The theologian has to take note of what science reveals at all the varied levels of explanation with which it works, because the work of the scientist is helping to elucidate a part of the theologian's subject-matter.

The theologian then can neither dictate to nor ignore the scientist. What he learns from him may show that he has been misconstruing the implications of his beliefs about God and of his religious experience. On the other hand he cannot be dictated to by the scientist. For the scientist also often misconstrues his scientific experience and his claims may prove to be more comprehensive than is warranted by the evidence. The work of Teilhard de Chardin (whatever detailed criticisms may very properly be made of it) has been a healthy phenomenon. For he has made some theologians realize that the fact of evolution must be taken seriously and that it affects our fundamental understanding of the nature of God. And he has made some scientists realize that there is a spiritual dimension in human experience which has to be taken seriously in any understanding of the world as a whole.

In general, then, there is no need for a head-on conflict between science and theology. Neither can there be total dissociation between the two, as long as theology maintains its proper claim to be about how the world is and not simply about different possible human attitudes to the world. But there will always be some degree of tension between the two and the precise points at which adjustment and revision is called for will be continuously shifting.

Even if it be true that there does not need to be any head-on collision between science and theology, it has to be acknowledged that in the eyes of many there does appear to be a very much greater degree of conflict than my account would lead one to expect. This is primarily a psychological matter. The achievements of science, in particular the great precision which the physical sciences are able to achieve, has a strong psychological appeal. It very easily gives rise to the belief that ideally all explanations ought to be like that. I have already argued that this does not logically follow. Explanations must be appropriate to the nature of what it is they are trying to explain. The greater the degree of abstraction from life in what one is setting out to explain, the greater the degree of precision it is possible to obtain. But I believe it is possible to go further than that. Not only is it not logically necessary that all explanations should conform to the model of mathematico-physical explanations, it is in fact logically impossible that they should do so. Every explanation involves an observer, someone who is doing the explaining. He cannot be the object of his own observation in precisely the way that other things are. His explanation cannot therefore be comprehensively of one kind. For he cannot explain himself and his observing in the same way that he explain the things outside himself that he observes. When, therefore, the theologian resists any attempt to reduce all explanation to explanation of a single kind, he does not do so on the basis of some special theological insight. He does so because of the inherently self-contradictory character of the notion.

The theologian then need not fear that he will be subjected to a take-over bid from some scientific monopolist. But this is no ground for complacency. I have already emphasized that he needs always to listen to and to learn from the particular findings of the various scientists. They have significance for his work, though that significance is usually very indirect. Modern cosmological theories about the origins of the physical universe, for example, are far less directly relevant to the theological doctrine of creation than has sometimes been claimed. But there are lessons also of a more general kind that he can profitably learn from the whole pattern of scientific work. Lord Ashby in a recent broadcast talk insisted that it is the way the scientist works rather than his particular findings that it is most vital for those who are not themselves scientists to understand. 'It doesn't matter a hoot', he declared, 'whether historians, literary critics or classical scholars can describe the second law of thermodynamics. What does matter . . . is how it comes about that everyone who can describe the second law of thermodynamics agrees that it is "true".[1] So for the theologian also it is a matter of importance to understand how the scientist sets about his tasks and how he achieves the kinds of result that he does. The objective rigour of scientific study has succeeded in clarifying many things that previously appeared mysterious. The theologian, as I have emphasized, cannot take over the precise method (or, more accurately, methods) of the various scientific disciplines and use them for his own purposes for which they may not be suited. But neither can he simply shrug off the general challenge that he ought to be offering explanations which will stand up to rigorous testing of whatever kind is appropriate to the subject-matter involved. More particularly this means he must not allow himself to fall back on an appeal to external authorities which are not themselves allowed to be called into question. Scientific work does not involve dispensing with authorities altogether; but the story of its origins and of its continued progress does involve refusing to accept any authority as absolutely sacrosanct. The theologian has to ask himself very carefully whether this is not an aspect of scientific method which is appropriate in his own discipline also.

The two primary forms of authority in Christian tradition have been the authority of the Church and of the Bible. It is not surprising if people who affirm a unique incarnation of God in a particular historical figure should also claim that there must exist some absolutely reliable authority to mediate the substance and significance of that incarnation to later ages. I give two examples of such reasoning, the one arguing for the infallibility of the Church, the other for that of the Bible. The first comes from Newman's famous *Essay on the Development of Christian Doctrine:*

Reasons shall be given in this section for concluding that, in proportion to the probability of true developments of doctrine and practice in the Divine Scheme, so is the probability also of the appointment in that scheme of an external authority to decide upon them, thereby separating them from the mass of mere human speculation, extravagance, corruption, and error, in and out of which they grow. This is the doctrine of the infallibility of

[1] *The Listener*, 21 August 1975.

the Church; for by infallibility I suppose is meant the power of deciding whether this, that, and a third, and any number of theological or ethical statements are true.[1]

The other is taken from a book by a Dutch Calvinist writer, J. N. Geldenhuys:

The fact *as such* that Jesus possesses supreme divine authority . . . gives us the assurance that the Lord of all authority would have seen to it that, through the working of his power, an adequate and completely reliable account of and an authentic proclamation concerning the significance of His life and work were written and preserved for the ages to come.[2]

Both arguments have a *prima facie* reasonableness about them. Granted the initial faith in the incarnation, there does seem to be an appropriateness in the idea of a fully reliable authority to record and sustain the fruits of that special divine event. But it is an argument of the same basic kind that I have ascribed to the opponents of Galileo and of Darwin. As in those cases, so here the argument needs to be tested by the facts. And when tested by the facts, it is shown to be false just as decisively as was that of the opponents of scientific discovery in the seventeenth and the nineteenth centuries.

In practice, the exercise of authority has been less absolute in character than these quotations would suggest. Not all branches of the Church have affirmed its infallibility, and when it has been affirmed the range of its operation has been very restricted. Individual conscience and private judgement have been allowed some place. Nor have all Christians affirmed the infallibility of Scripture. And when it has been affirmed, the need for interpretation has in fact made possible a greater variety of belief than might on the face of it have seemed likely. Nevertheless, the basic idea has been a characteristic of Christian tradition down the ages. There has been an underlying conviction that in the official declaration of the teaching Church properly understood, or in the Scriptures properly interpreted, there are accessible to man truths

[1] J. H. Newman, *An Essay on the Development of Christian Doctrine* (New York, 1960), p. 97.
[2] J. N. Geldenhuys, *Supreme Authority* (London, 1953), p. 43.

about God which can be known to be true beyond all question because of the authoritative source from which they come.

It is the belief that theology functions in this authoritative way which is the primary ground for attacks upon it from many of its leading intellectual opponents. I give two examples. Freud's famous book, *The Future of an Illusion*, is more of a general attack upon authoritarianism in religion from a broadly scientific point of view than a careful critique from a specifically psychological standpoint. In the course of it he contrasts the teachings of religion with other teachings and asserts that in the case of the former 'it is forbidden to raise the question of their authentication at all'.[1] The philosopher Nowell-Smith makes a similar criticism in the moral sphere in the course of a discussion of the notion that the fundamental sin is disobedience to God. He writes:

The idea of heteronomy is also strongly marked in Christian morality: 'Not as I will, but as thou wilt'. The demand made by Christianity is that of surrendering self, not in the ordinary sense of being unselfish, of loving our neighbour and even our enemy. It is the total surrender of the *will* that is required; Abraham must be prepared to sacrifice Isaac at God's command, and I take this to mean that we must be prepared to sacrifice our most deeply felt moral concerns if God should require us to do so. If we dare to ask why, the only answer is 'Have faith'; and faith is an essentially heteronomous idea; for it is not a reasoned trust in someone in whom we have good grounds for reposing trust; it is blind faith, utter submission of our own reason and will.[2]

There are aspects of the Christian tradition which give some justification for these protests. It is not only obviously debased forms of Christian faith which have left themselves open to this kind of objection. Kierkegaard, for example, uses the story of Abraham and Isaac in just the way that Nowell-Smith castigates.[3] But the protest is also to be heard

---

[1] S. Freud, *Future of an Illusion* (London, 1962), p. 22.

[2] P. H. Nowell-Smith, 'Morality: Religious and Secular', in ed. I. T. Ramsey, *Christian Ethics and Contemporary Philosophy* (London, 1966), p. 104.

[3] See S. Kierkegaard, *Fear and Trembling*, Problem I (cited by K. Ward, *Ethics and Christianity* (London, 1970), p. 162).

from within Christianity itself. In Dostoevsky's vision, it is Christ himself who is seen as diametrically opposed to any such idea; it is the returned Christ figure with whom the Grand Inquisitor is remonstrating when he declares: 'We have corrected Thy work and have founded it upon *miracle*, *mystery* and *authority* . . . Why has Thou come now to hinder us?'[1] Bonhoeffer's much quoted and much misunderstood phrase, 'man come of age', was essentially a protest against the idea that the Christian could or should be freed from responsible decision by submission to external authority.

But such protests, valid as they are, do not do away with the concept of authority in religion altogether. How then ought it to be understood? It is at this point, I believe, that there is much to be learnt from the way in which the scientific community functions. There is such a thing as scientific orthodoxy. A great proportion of what any scientist believes at any given time is accepted by him on authority—the authority both of the past and of contemporary scholars. He has no option. He must do so if he is to have a general framework of knowledge of a kind that is essential for any further advances in science. This acceptance of an orthodox tradition is, then, both inevitable and obviously beneficial. But it does have its dangers. It makes the acceptance of radically new ideas much more difficult. This has often happened. The first accounts of hypnotism, for example, were vigorously disputed by the orthodoxy of the day. The initial opposition to both Galileo and Darwin was not exclusively on religious grounds; scientific orthodoxy was also largely hostile at first. But within the scientific community it is accepted in theory, and in the long run in practice too, that all scientific knowledge, however authoritatively received from the past, is open to revision. The tests that are necessary to show convincingly the validity of such new ways of seeing things as that proposed by Copernicus in the sixteenth century or by the proponents of extra-sensory perception in our own, are enormously complex. In the early stages there are usually alternative hypotheses available to account for the new phenomena,

---

[1] F. Dostoevsky, *The Brothers Karamazov* (trans. Constance Garnett), p. 264.

which, if slightly forced in themselves, have the obvious advantage of leaving large tracts of apparently well-established knowledge undisturbed. But however well-established that knowledge, it is not absolute. In the course of time it can be and frequently has been subjected to change and to revision.

Theology need not necessarily function in precisely the same way. But the parallel may be of help to the theologian in his attempt to see the positive, but non-authoritarian, rôle of authority in religion. For the Christian the only absolute authority is God. This principle is of political importance in opposition to tyranny. There is a point at which the prophetic protest may have to be made: 'We must obey God rather than men' (Acts 5:29). To allow an absolute claim to any person or theory within the finite world is a form of idolatry. 'If any one comes to me,' says Jesus, 'and does not hate his own father and mother and wife and children and brothers and sisters, yea, and even his own life, he cannot be my disciple' (Luke 14:26). The point of the saying is not that family ties and family affection are bad things; indeed, if that were so, the saying would lose its point. It is precisely because they are the highest of human goods that they are in danger of being given an absoluteness that belongs to God alone.

This principle applies to the realm of beliefs also. Any putative authority in the matter of religious belief that makes absolute claims for itself has become an idol. And the more valuable and sacred a thing it is in its true nature, the greater the danger that it may come to claim absoluteness for itself or to have absoluteness thrust upon it. But if it does, it has become an idol. Thus it is precisely because the Church and the Bible are so vital to Christian faith that the danger of treating them as absolute authorities is so insidious. They are not absolute; but they are authorities of the utmost importance for religion and for theology. How then do they function as authorities?

Legal authority is capable of settling things decisively. In certain circumstances a judge or parliament may make an authoritative decision and from that moment on what has been decided is in fact law. Had the relevant authority decided the other way it would not have been law. Churches, as institutions, have a legal aspect. In certain circumstances they can decide what is to be the constitution or the practices or even the official beliefs of that particular institution. Such decisions may be legally binding and historically decisive but they cannot be theologically binding or decisive. Authority in theology cannot operate in that judicial manner. The scientific parallel is much more apposite than the legal. Like the scientific community, the Church embodies the wisdom of the past in its religious practice and its religious thought. It encapsulates that wisdom so as to make it available to new situations and for the teaching of future generations. With the Church as with science the provision of such a framework of generally accepted belief and practice is an essential prerequisite to any growth in the realm either of practice or of understanding. But that framework must be open to revision. The good teacher does not see himself as simply passing on a fixed deposit of knowledge to be kept intact like the one talent, safely wrapped in its napkin. He sees himself rather as providing the framework of knowledge and experience within which new discoveries can be made. He hopes for new light to come from those he has taught, which will lead to corrections and improvements in what he himself has believed and handed on.

The way in which the Bible functions as an authority for the Christian theologian is varied and complex. In part its authority is comparable to that of essential evidence in historical study. For it is fundamental to any understanding of the figure of Jesus, of that from which he emerged and of that to which his life gave rise. But it is not simply a matter of historical evidence. It embodies religious insight and religious interpretation of the greatest profundity and challenge. In neither respect is its contribution either uniform in character or exclusive of all other. Not all the historical witness of the Bible is of equal worth, nor does it contain all that is needed for a full understanding of the significance of Jesus. The religious quality of its writings is also variable and there are other writings of a religious stature comparable with many of the books of the Bible. The exact boundaries of the canon are a matter of historical contingency. What we have is not a collection of writings all of which are clearly different in character from any writing not so included. We have a collection which at an early stage the Church decided to regard as its foundation documents and which have constituted an important common ground in the thought and devotion of the Church ever since. We have already considered in our earlier account of biblical studies some of the problems involved in a properly critical use of the Bible. But for all the need of such strictly critical appraisal, it remains an essential authority for the theologian. It is authoritative in a way that combines something of the authority which fundamental documentary evidence has for the historian with that which a great creative work of art has for the literary or artistic tradition that stems from it.

The Anglican tradition has often tried to do justice to the Christian's critical use of his authorities by speaking of the threefold authority of Bible, Church, and reason. The point being made is important, the way of making it is not wholly satisfactory. Reason is not so much a separate authority; it is a way of using one's authorities. The Bible and the Church are two important authorities for the theologian, though they are not the only ones which he uses. But the vital point is how he uses them. He does not search them for ready-made answers, like those to be found at the back of a mathematical textbook. He uses them as sources which are of indispensable help to him in the task of determining what as a Christian theologian he should properly affirm. As in the case of the scientist, all his authorities are secondary authorities. They provide him with a range of evidence beyond his own experience and that of his immediate circle. They show him what patterns of interpretation have proved fruitful and creative in the past. Thereby they free him in some measure from the arbitrariness of his own limited perspective. But they do not relieve him of the responsibility of making his own assessments and his own judgement.

2. THE HUMAN SCIENCES

I have argued that the theologian cannot ignore the findings of the natural scientist because in elucidating the nature of the world that we inhabit, the scientist is elucidating the nature of what is a part of the theologian's subject-matter. But the theologian is particularly concerned with man, with his inner life and with his life in community. The more therefore the scientist is concerned with the study of human life, the more directly his work impinges on the work of the theologian. I want, therefore, to turn now to those two branches of science which deal most directly with man's inner life and his life in society—psychology and sociology.

It is in the more theoretical and speculative aspects of these subjects that their most obvious links with the work of theology are to be found. At that level they seek to offer generalized accounts of the ways in which men come to hold particular beliefs or to adopt particular social customs. There the interrelation with theological accounts is particularly close. But many psychologists and sociologists are themselves highly suspicious of such generalized approaches. In practice much of the work done in these two fields today is of an experimental kind, dealing with specific and narrowly-defined issues. Such experimental work contributes to the work of the theologian in the same limited way that the work of the natural scientist does, though with an increased intensity because of the concentration of its attention on human behaviour. But even though the impact of such work, treated piecemeal, may be very restricted, that should not lead us to underestimate its significance when treated as a whole. For however much experimental psychologists and sociologists may eschew more general theorizing their work embodies an approach to human knowledge and a perspective on human life which it is of the utmost importance for the theologian to grasp. Its bearing on theology may be indirect, but it is also very profound.

The theories and methods of psychologists are almost as varied as those of theologians. This adds to the difficulty of speaking in general terms about the relation between the two subjects. At its simplest and most popular level the claim may sometimes be heard that psychology undermines the validity of theology as a form of knowledge by showing it to be the product of wish-fulfilment. The argument can be developed in much more sophisticated forms, but it can be given appropriately popular illustration by the citation of Rupert Brooke's entertaining poem, *Heaven*.[1]

> Fish (fly-replete, in depth of June,
> Dawdling away their wat'ry noon)
> Ponder deep wisdom, dark or clear,
> Each secret fishy hope or fear.
> Fish say, they have their Stream and Pond;
> But is there anything Beyond?
> This life cannot be All, they swear,
> For how unpleasant, if it were!
> One may not doubt that, somehow, Good
> Shall come of Water and of Mud;
> And, sure, the reverent eye must see
> A Purpose in Liquidity.
> We darkly know, by Faith we cry,
> The future is not Wholly Dry.
> Mud unto mud!—Death eddies near—
> Not here the appointed End, not here!
> But somewhere, beyond Space and Time,
> Is wetter water, slimier slime!
> And there (they trust) there swimmeth One
> Who swam ere rivers were begun,
> Immense, of fishy form and mind,
> Squamous, omnipotent, and kind;
> And under that Almighty Fin,
> The littlest fish may enter in.
> Oh! never fly conceals a hook,
> Fish say, in the Eternal Brook,
> But more than mundane weeds are there,
> And mud, celestially fair;
> Fat caterpillars drift around,
> And Paradisal grubs are found;
> Unfading moths, immortal flies,
> And the worm that never dies.

[1] R. Brooke, *Collected Poems* (London, 1936), pp. 130-1.

And in that Heaven of all their wish,
There shall be no more land, say fish.

Man has fashioned God in his own image in order to satisfy his own desires. The argument is not to be lightly dismissed. It is impossible to deny the human capacity for fantasy-building where there is no corresponding reality. Few would want to question that such processes have contributed to the particular forms taken by some religious beliefs. May it not also be the source of religious belief as a whole? It remains a possibility and one's assessment of the issue will depend in part on one's evaluation of the other types of argument for the reality of God that we have already touched upon.[1] But the argument is bound to remain inconclusive. The evidence can perfectly well be accounted for by the converse explanation: God has made man in his own image, and those wishes or desires, which on the other explanation are the ground of man's creating God in his image, are there precisely because man is made in God's image. 'Thou has made us towards thyself,' said Augustine, 'and our hearts are restless till they find their rest in thee.' However great the care and the detail with which this line of thought is developed, the evidence is inescapably ambivalent; it can always be interpreted either way.

This is the inevitable fate of attempting to press a psychological explanation into service beyond its proper rôle. Psychological explanations of this kind are concerned to clarify the processes by which men have come to hold certain beliefs. While that question may well have some bearing on any attempt to judge the truth or falsity of those beliefs, it cannot by itself be determinative of the issue. Let us illustrate the point with a simple example. A man is in love with a girl, but there is a rival on the scene. He regards his rival as mean, scheming, and worthless, but tells himself that his judgement is unreliable since it may be distorted by jealousy. (Alternatively he may regard his rival as dazzlingly handsome and attractive, but similarly regard that judgement as unreliable for the same reason.) His judgement may indeed be false,

[1] See pp. 50–7 above.

but it is not necessarily so however great his jealousy. It may be that his judgement is entirely valid and his emotional involvement has simply made him much more observant of what is really going on than he would otherwise have been. The recognition of the involvement of his own jealousy in the situation ought not to lead him to abandon his initial judgement forthwith. It ought however to make him question it, to make him look again at the reasons for it and to reassess them with an ultra-critical eye.

If then we meet with the claim that psychological explanation can show the theologian's affirmation to be false, we must enter a strong demurrer. But the fact that such explanations may on occasion be pressed in this illegitimate way does not preclude them from embodying a genuine challenge to the work of theology that needs to be taken very seriously.

The link between religion and wish-fulfilment is particularly associated with the name of Freud and it is instructive to note his own handling of the argument. He defined an illusion as a belief to which wish-fulfilment has contributed, whether that belief itself be true or false. To call religion an illusion did not therefore automatically imply its falsity. It implied only that wish-fulfilment contributes to it and that for that reason its beliefs need to have the support of exceptionally good reasons if they are to be maintained as true. And this was precisely what Freud felt to be lacking. 'We should not', he wrote, 'be able to bring ourselves to accept anything of so little concern to us as the fact that whales bear young instead of laying eggs, if it were not capable of better proof than this.'[1] If Freud meant to suggest that the 'proofs' for religious belief ought to be of the same kind as those applicable to the reproductive mechanism of whales, his argument, for reasons that have already been outlined, is a thoroughly bad one. If, on the other hand, he means only to insist on the importance of reasons in a sphere where our deepest feelings are involved, his warning is salutary.

The same point has been made in lively style by H. A. Williams in an essay entitled 'The God I want'. In it he writes:

[1] S. Freud, op. cit., p. 23.

. . . the cumulative evidence produced by Freud and Jung for the rationalization of unrecognized desire is so overwhelming that it can no longer be ignored. And it compels careful scrutiny of any claim that I know what is the case rather than what I want to be the case. This is true even in the field of natural science. Darwin said he was aware of it and did all he could to counteract it. But laboratory experiments, the disciplined observation of what happens, is a bulwark against rationalization in the field of scientific method. Only when a scientist turns philosopher, expounding a world-view in terms of his own particular scientific investigation, does the exorcized ghost of rationalization reappear to disguise what is wanted in the garments of objective truth. It is almost inevitable when we are concerned with what cannot be subject to controlled experiment. Here the field is wide open for making my assertion of what is wait upon what I want, and this without knowing what I am doing. Suppose, for instance, that what I want above all else is security. I may be only dimly aware of this overmastering desire, or not aware of it at all. What I am perhaps painfully aware of are much more superficial and transient desires like those for professional success or sexual gratification. Powerful though these may sometimes be, how can I allow such whims and fancies to influence my understanding of what is? That indeed would be building upon sand. So I hanker after a knowledge independent of them. If I am religious and have an enquiring mind, I hanker after what is called an objective theology—a description of God and His ways with men which has nothing to do with my desire to be a bishop and to sleep with Betty. So far, so good. A description of God controlled by these kinds of concupiscence would indeed be worthless. What, however, is hidden from me is my deeper, permanent, but hidden desire to live in an impregnable intellectual fortress, safe from attack by any and every wind of change. If I am emotionally and intellectually naïve, this may lead me to adopt a biblical fundamentalism. If I am more sophisticated, my desire for security will have to clothe itself with longer and more sophisticated arguments. I may read and think myself into a Thomist or a Barthian. What I do not perceive is that, for all the claims to be the servant of an objective theology, what I have really obtained is the God I want. For the God I want is the God who appears to be independent of what I want. My dislike or fear of spiritual adventure, my desire above all to feel safe, has led me to buy a commodity which claims to deliver me from such adventure and to give me such safety. And the commodity so bought is precisely the God I want. However little, if at all, I am able to see through the trick, it is my subjective feelings which have led me to choose the article advertised as objective.[1]

Williams comes very near to saying that the rationalization of desire is so determinative of man's beliefs that in the area of theology at least it is the only effective force at work. I have already given reasons for suggesting that that would be an unwarranted and exaggerated claim. Nevertheless, if exaggeration, it is exaggeration of something real and pervasive. Religion is certainly an area where the dangers of self-deception are great. Recognition of that fact is one reason why there is so deep-seated a desire to find a fully reliable and objective authority in Church or Bible. But we have already seen that no such fully reliable external authority is available for our use. If then we eschew such appeals, as we are bound to do, what recourse is open to us? Any claim that some specific religious belief must be true because of its inherently self-authenticating character is particularly vulnerable in the face of the psychologist's observations. I have already argued that theology is a matter of the responsible assessment of evidence, and our discussion of psychology so far has reinforced the need for this. But I have also had to acknowledge already that the criteria appropriate to such assessments are extremely difficult to determine, and in view of this fact we have to admit that the dangers to which Freud and Williams point are very real. We ought not to regard them as destructive of the whole enterprise, but neither should we take them lightly. How then should we proceed in proper recognition of them?

Let us begin by looking a bit more closely at the way in which the psychological processes by which men come to hold their religious beliefs may have contributed to the content of those beliefs. And let us for that purpose assume the truth of the highly plausible hypothesis that projection of the parent figure is a part of the psychological mechanism which has enabled men to form and to affirm belief in God. This

[1] In ed. J. Mitchell, *The God I Want* (London, 1967), pp. 167-8.

assumption does not of itself, as we have seen, carry any suggestion that there is in fact no divine reality corresponding to the God in whom men have come with the help of this process to believe. It would seem natural on this assumption that the nature of the parent figure actually experienced would tend to colour a person's conception of the nature of God. The offspring of a strict, masterful and somewhat distant patriarchal figure, characteristic of some Victorian households such as the Barretts of Wimpole Street, might be expected to develop a conception of God of a comparably stern and forbidding character. There is some experimental evidence to suggest that this sort of thing does in fact happen. It was found, for example, 'in a cross-cultural study of sixty-five primitive societies, that where child-rearing was nurturant, the gods were regarded as benevolent, but when child-rearing was punitive, the gods were seen as malevolent'.[1]

If there is even a tendency for this kind of thing to happen, how should the theologian allow for it in the critical assessment of religious belief? The experience of fatherhood of any single individual, or indeed of any particular society, is bound to be limited; it will include certain possibilities but others will be necessarily absent. Should the theologian then abandon the 'father' image altogether in any more serious and systematic talk about God, on the ground that what it conveys to people will be determined more by the variety of their experiences of earthly fatherhood than by the reality of divine fatherhood itself? If he were to do so, he would soon find himself faced with similar grounds for abandoning all images with reference to God. He would then be left with no analogical ground for his speech about God at all. He would be forced to become a strict adherent of the *via negativa*—or abandon theology altogether.

An alternative course is that he should extend the range of his images so that they will be mutually corrective of one another. This is a familiar characteristic of religious language. The hymn-writer revels in a variety of imagery:

[1] M. Argyle, 'Seven Psychological Roots of Religion', *Theology*, LXVII, August 1964, p. 336.

Jesus, my Shepherd, Husband, Friend,
My Prophet, Priest and King,
My Lord, my Life, my Way, my End,
Accept the praise I bring.[1]

The theologian feels a proper urge to tidy up the profusion of images, but he has to learn that he cannot systematize to a greater degree than his subject-matter allows. We have already seen how, for philosophical reasons, his language about God is bound to be indirect and inexact; this need for varied imagery is reinforced by a recognition of the psychological limitations and distortions that are bound to affect the significance of particular images for specific individuals or societies. Theology is rooted in the ordinary experience of men and women and must not lose touch with it. But it is not simply a reflection of that experience, it seeks always to extend and to transcend it.

So far we have been concerned with a primarily Freudian approach to religious belief and to beliefs about God in particular. I want now to consider in an even more general way the broad implications of the stress which most psychologists lay on the rôle of unconscious processes in relation to the determination of belief. Different schools understand the unconscious in enormously varied ways, but few would deny its great importance in every area of fundamental belief. Men do not work out their primary beliefs by a straightforward process of rational decision. Many of our basic belief systems are, of course, taken over uncritically in the first instance from our parents and from society. But even the process of critical reflection upon them cannot be fully understood in terms of rational and conscious processes. There are basic drives at work within men at a level of which they are not consciously aware. One important way in which these unconscious processes find expression is through symbolism. Symbols can be used to co-ordinate the chaos of experience in ways which surmount logical or emotional incompatibility and they may do so without our being conscious of the meaning that they embody. In such cases we may accept

[1] English Hymnal, No. 405.

beliefs, not because we have understood them, tested them, and found them to be true, but rather because through them certain basic drives within ourselves find expression of a kind which enables us to come to terms with them and to cope with them.

We have already made some reference to symbols in our discussion of language about God. What is now being suggested is that such symbolism may be giving expression to more fundamental psychological processes than its discussion in the context of religious language might suggest. Recognition of processes of this kind is essential if the work of theology is not to be interpreted in a misleadingly cerebral manner. It is particularly important for any adequate approach to sacramental theology, but it applies to the whole range of doctrinal affirmations. I will try to illustrate the general principle by indicating points at which it may be important for the doctrines of the eucharist and of death and resurrection.

The eucharist is central to Christian worship. One basic reason for that is its institution, or belief in its institution, by Jesus: 'Do this in remembrance of me.' But Jesus did not simply invent it from scratch, and neither have Christians valued it simply as an act of obedience and historical imitation. Whether the Last Supper was a passover meal or not, Jesus was drawing upon a tradition of religious meals which had been characteristic of Judaism for centuries. And these in their turn were one particular form of an almost universal custom of giving religious significance to a shared meal. Certain basic social human needs seem to lie behind the custom and to find satisfaction through it. But the Christian eucharist is a particular version of this widespread custom and there are special meanings associated with it. These cannot be understood apart from the history of Jesus, but there is more to be said about them than simply a recounting of the historical links. In the eucharist the Christian is said to feed upon the body of Christ. One can trace the historical origins of that notion, but may it not be just as significant to see in it a link with a fundamental human urge, epitomized by the infant drawing its vital sustenance from the body of its mother? Or, again, in the eucharist the Christian is said to be made one with Christ, as the bread becomes for him the body of Christ and is taken, by eating, into his own. Here too there are surely links with deep-seated drives towards union with the beloved of a social, and especially a sexual, kind. Psychology's understanding of these aspects of human life is both limited and speculative. But without attention to them Christian understanding of the eucharist is likely to be seriously impoverished.

Similarly Christian conversion is spoken of in terms of death and resurrection. Here too there is a primary historical reference to the death and resurrection of Christ. But that is not the whole story. Language of death and resurrection is frequently encountered in purely psychological accounts of the process of human maturation. The psychologist's language has, of course, been influenced by the Christian tradition at this point. But it may also be that Christian insistence on death and resurrection as language appropriate to religious conversion owes something to its conformity with fundamental patterns of human maturation. It is an area in which theology and psychology may be mutually illuminating.

A final illustration is the important rôle played by the figure of the Virgin Mary in Christian tradition. On scriptural and historical grounds the cult of the Virgin has very weak foundations, as protestant critics have not been slow to point out. But equally evidently its symbolic power is enormous. It appears to correspond to some basic human need which does not find adequate expression at any other point in Christian belief or worship. Williams has spoken of the Virgin as a 'symbol of that aspect of God's love which can only be conveyed to us by means of a feminine analogy'.[1] And Jung described the Trinity as 'of an exclusively masculine character' and spoke of an unconscious tendency to transform it into a quaternity by the addition of a female principle, such as the Mother of God.[2]

[1] H. A. Williams, 'Theology and Self-Awareness' in ed. A. Vidler, *Soundings* (Cambridge, 1962), p. 100.

[2] C. G. Jung, *Psychology and Religion* (Newhaven, 1938), pp. 76-7.

This last example may serve to show the difficulty which faces the theologian in deciding how to handle this kind of psychological insight. Christianity is not simply an imaginative weaving together of psychologically powerful symbols. It has a given historical element. The theologian needs to recognize that part of the spiritual power of that history is dependent on the universal symbolism to which it gives expression. Moreover the Church is free to contribute to the shape of its own historical development with the help of such psychological insights into the character of its past. But it is not free to do just whatever it likes with its historical inheritance. It has to take seriously the happenedness of the past. So theology must pay attention to history as well as to psychology in determining its own proper procedures. But before taking up the implications of historical study for theology, something must be said about the second of our human sciences—sociology.

The Christian who emphasizes the primacy of personal faith or who defines religion as 'the flight of the alone to the Alone' is likely to look upon psychology as the study most directly related to theology. But religion is an essentially social phenomenon. It is true that the Roman authorities were puzzled by Christianity in its early days because, unlike Judaism, it was not the religion of a clearly-defined national group. But it was nonetheless a social movement from the outset. Personal faith in Christ and membership of the Church went absolutely hand in hand with one another. Even the Reformation protest against the institutionalized faith of the Catholic church gave rise not simply to numbers of individual Christians but rather to a variety of denominations and sects. These too were powerful social entities though they functioned in a way very different from that of the Catholic church. This is not to suggest that the social situation always determines what a man's beliefs will be. There is always scope for an Athanasius *contra mundum*. But religious belief can never be properly understood except in close relation to the social situation in which it functions.

Sociology then is likely to prove every bit as significant for the theologian as psychology. Indeed it stands to theology in fundamentally the same kind of relation as does psychology. There is in sociology as in psychology a continuing flow of experimental work of a highly specific kind, which is of interest to the work of theology but which is too detailed for consideration here. There are also broader, more generalized accounts of the characteristic functioning of different types of society. Some of these have given special attention to the rôle played by religion within society. It is with a very brief review of some of these that I wish to begin, before going on to consider some of the ways in which the insights that they provide may be of significance for the theologian in his own work.

Sociological accounts of religion are more likely to be put forward today as complete explanations of religion than psychological accounts. It needs therefore to be said briefly at the outset that it is in principle impossible for them to fulfil that rôle. The reasons are essentially the same as in the case of psychology. Sociology can give some of the reasons (though never anything like a complete account) why particular societies have adopted particular religious beliefs and practices, and it can provide an account of the social function that religion has fulfilled in those societies. But the patterns that it reveals are nothing like regular enough or universal enough to support a claim to be complete explanations, doing away with any need for explanations of other kinds. In giving, therefore, a very brief outline of three classical approaches to religion of a broadly sociological kind, I do not expect to have to take very seriously any claim that they constitute disproof of the validity of distinctively religious or theological beliefs.

But even though such extreme claims can be disposed of comparatively easily, this does not undermine the importance of such approaches for the theologian. The fact that such an all-embracing rôle has on occasion been ascribed to them suggests that at the very least they must be describing important aspects of the social rôle played by religious beliefs. And if that indeed proves to be the case, the theologian needs to ask whether the insights that such accounts provide may not require of him careful reconsideration and perhaps even revision of the form that such beliefs should properly take.

Marx regarded all religious belief as fallacious. This conviction was rooted in his dialectical materialist beliefs which he held primarily on philosophical grounds. But what was important to him was the way in which religion had arisen in response to certain needs within society and the function that it fulfilled there. Marx's view has points of similarity to the Freudian theory of projection. For Marx saw religion as arising out of a sense of deprivation. Alienated from the social order, which they have in fact themselves created, men seek compensation in a fantasy world. But it is an inverted world that man creates in the heavens. For God is an absolute ruler who has ordained man's place in the world and in society— the exact opposite in Marx's view of the real relation between men and their rulers. The social results of this fantasy construction are twofold. On the one hand it offers compensation for the oppressed; it is the 'opium of the people'. On the other hand it also provides a justification for the existing social order. Both aspects of its influence therefore act against the possibility of social change. Marx did not deny that the religious impulse at times has involved a genuine cry of the oppressed with revolutionary potential; such indeed was for him a characteristic feature of Christianity at its inception. But as soon as religion develops its other-worldly character, it can serve only to confirm the situation of oppression. If therefore there is to be any social change the influence of religion has to be got out of the way.

That religion in general, and the Christianity of Marx's day in particular, has tended to fulfil such a rôle is undeniable. But that this is true of all religion with an other worldly emphasis is hard to support. Prophetic religion, with its appeal to the transcendent majesty of God, has not infrequently played a diametrically opposite rôle and constituted a disruptive challenge to the existing social order. Marx's theory points to an important feature of the way religion has often functioned in society, but not to something which is universally true of religion as such.

The French sociologist, Emile Durkheim, affirms the

closest possible links between religion and society. Religion for him was not, as for Marx, an unfortunate by-product of the social process. It is, and always has been, something fundamental to society itself. In his most important work, *The Elementary Forms of the Religious Life*, he set out to study the most primitive example of a religious system available. There he found the realm of the sacred (for him the distinctive characteristic of all religion) to be coterminous with society. It served to provide a focus of common identity which is essential to the cohesive functioning of any community. In a communal society of a comparatively simple structure, like a village community or a nomadic tribe, where environmental conditions make it essential for the whole community to act together for all purposes, it is particularly vital. Modern western society, by contrast, is a much more complex and fragmented phenomenon. Men's social existence is not a single, unified thing. They exercise it by belonging to a variety of loose associations—a place of work, a political party, a golf club, a local pub. Each of these has its own centre of unity and each makes only restricted claims on the allegiance of its members. In such a setting, religion is no longer needed to play the unifying rôle that it fulfilled in less diversified forms of society. So today Christianity plays a much less central rôle in Western European society than it has done in the past. Yet even so it does not show signs of disappearing as completely as Durkheim's account might lead us to expect, were it a fully adequate account of the reasons for the phenomenon of religion.

The German sociologist, Max Weber, also gave religion a fundamental rôle in securing the cohesiveness of society, though in a form which does more justice to the facts of social and religious change. What he emphasized was the myth-making character of religion, whereby it was able to provide society with a common pattern of overall meaning. This has been of particular importance in enabling men to make some sense of such eventualities as suffering and death by placing them within a wider context of meaning. Thus the essential character of religion's rôle in social terms was the provision of human signification to life in the world on a comprehensive scale. Moreover on that score Christianity may have to be described as having done its job too well. The religious sense of an ordered and intelligible world, most fully expressed in Thomism, helped to pave the way for the development of scientific thought. So alternative patterns of meaning of a scientific kind were developed and the function which religion had fulfilled in the past has been extensively taken over by other, more rationalistic interpretations of the world.

I have already argued that none of these (or other comparable) accounts can rightly claim to contribute an all-embracing explanation of religion but that that fact does not absolve the theologian from paying serious attention to them. The extremely brief outlines that I have given of them are designed simply to indicate in a more concrete form the kind of approach to be found in such sociological studies of religion. We need now to ask how such sociological insights apply to the particular development of Christianity. In what ways have social factors contributed to its history and to its thought? There can be no doubt that they have played a substantial part in determining what communities have accepted the gospel at particular times and what precise form Christianity has taken in those communities. I have already pointed to the importance of recognizing such factors in the work of Church history and cited the Donatist movement in North Africa as one illustration.[1] It is a principle that has clearly been operative throughout religious history. The early development of Israelite religion in the Old Testament provides obvious examples. Many of the prophets looked to the desert period as the time when Israel was most faithful to Yahweh. The demanding conditions of her nomadic life at that stage required a close-knit community with an intense spirit of mutual loyalty and dedication. This had provided the setting within which the high, if sometimes harsh and exclusive, morality for which the prophets stood, had come to birth. The more settled agricultural life of Palestine posed different needs; these were reflected in the traditional Baal worship of Canaan which for all the prophets' condemnation of it also made a positive contribution

[1] See pp. 40–1 above.

to the evolving religion of Israel. And so it has always been. The Christianity that has been characteristic of the Negro peoples of America, for example, and the contemporary development of a 'theology of liberation' in South America are clearly linked with the social problems of those particular situations.

Once the theologian has recognized such links, how ought he to assess them? He ought not to look upon them with regret as so many distortions of the true faith. Just as theology must express itself psychologically through the imagery and the experience of particular people and groups, limited and one-sided though that may be, so, since Christianity is a way of life, its expression ought to bear a positive relationship to the various social situations in which men find themselves. It should adapt its form so that it is clearly related to the underlying problems with which a society is faced, and can help men to make sense of their lives within it. But can it do so without becoming just a reflection of what that society already is? How can we distinguish between creative adaptation on the one hand and self-destructive compromise on the other? I want to approach this problem by illustration of some of the ways in which the problem has arisen in the recent history of the Church.

I take as my first illustration some reflections on the doctrine of the Church and ministry, which were central to the critique of the Roman Catholic Church made by Charles Davis in his book, *A Question of Conscience*, written to explain his renunciation of his priesthood, but which are also applicable beyond the confines of that particular communion. The hierarchical structure of the Church—the papacy, bishops, priests, and so forth—was a natural development in a world which conceived of men as having a fixed place in society. Within that social context it may have been the necessary form of order to enable the Church to reflect and to express Christian truth that would relate effectively to the whole fabric of men's lives. But this ecclesiastical structure, which was in part at least determined by the social conditions of the time, came to be regarded as something fixed. It was given a historical and theological justification, and treated as an essential and unchanging element of faith. Meanwhile the patterns of the surrounding society have changed. They allow for much greater social mobility, much greater varieties of individual development, new conceptions of human relationships within society. In the very different setting of the modern world, the hierarchical structure of the Church takes on a very different look. A pattern that at one time provided an appropriate setting for the furtherance of the Christian gospel, may by the very fact of not having changed tend to produce repression and the impoverishment of Christian life. Just as property laws, which achieved the desirable results of increasing productivity and ensuring equity between individuals in an agrarian society, may do precisely the reverse if left to operate unaltered in an industrial society, so the life of the Church cannot simply ignore changes in society without disastrous consequences. Such an account does not of course include all the factors that need to be considered in determining a Christian doctrine of the ministry. Historical and other factors are also relevant. Moreover important changes have taken place in the actual functioning of the ministry even where the basic framework has been treated as unchangeable. But it does show the dangers that are likely to attend theological argument that fails to take serious note of the social factors.

It is not only in such obvious cases as church order that social factors are relevant. They are operative over the whole range of doctrinal beliefs. In some famous lectures delivered in 1900, the great German scholar, Adolf Harnack, set out to expound the 'essence of Christianity'. What he there put forward as Christianity's continuing and unchanging essence was the fatherhood of God and the infinite value of the human soul. He recognized the apocalyptic element in Jesus' preaching but regarded that as something he shared with his contemporaries and which was of less continuing significance for Christianity. The later developments of christological dogma and the importance ascribed to it for man's redemption was in his eyes a distortion of the true Gospel. Now Harnack was not only the outstanding Church historian of his day, but also a leading figure in the general cultural life

of Germany. And many of his critics saw in his selection of
what was essential to Christianity the work not so much of
Harnack the historian as of Harnack the apostle of German
culture. The strongest and most effective reaction to his
approach was the movement initiated by the publication of
Karl Barth's Commentary on the Epistle to the Romans in
1919, with its stress on the utter inadequacy of the human
mind to grasp the reality of the living God. This in its turn
has with equal propriety been interpreted as something
partly brought about by the cultural shock of the First World
War.[1]

But it is always easier to criticize work in this kind of way
than it is to provide an alternative. One particularly interest-
ing reaction to Harnack's attempt to expound the 'essence of
Christianity' was that of Ernst Troeltsch, who had been
much influenced by Max Weber. He insisted that the relation
of Christianity to culture always was and should be recipro-
cal. Christianity was always part of an organic whole, and
there was no unchanging essence of doctrine to be extracted
from it. Theology was therefore chasing a will-o-the-wisp if it
attempted to find a set of unchanging beliefs that were the
distinctive mark of Christianity at all times. Any such account
was bound to be both superficial and misleading. The proper
task of theology was rather to describe the changing historical
phenomenon of the Church, depicting its life and thought as
they found concrete expression in the very varied conditions
of each succeeding epoch. It should not expect to find any
identical substratum of beliefs running right through that
story, for Christianity itself was a changing phenomenon. To
understand Christianity properly was to see it in the varying
forms that it has actually existed in differing social and
cultural situations.

We may take an illustration of this general position from
the doctrine of the atonement. Central to the Christian gospel
is the message that in Christ God has by his grace done what
was needed to meet the fundamental predicament of man and
and to make available to him a way of escape from it. But

[1] See pp. 45–6 above.

that remains a purely formal account apart from some more specific account of the nature of that predicament and of the salvation from it. These have been very differently understood in different ages. And those differences have related to differences in the social situation of the times. At one level this can be seen as no more than a difference of imagery drawn from differing social conditions—redemption in an age of slavery, expiation of man's offence in a feudal age, and the overcoming of alienation in an age of social and cultural fragmentation. But the differences have gone deeper than that. They can be seen as more than mere changes of clothing for the same message. For man's predicament has not merely been understood in differing terminology. Socially speaking it has actually been different. And since man's salvation relates not merely to some future life but also to a transformation of the human situation now, the message itself has been different. Any talk about man's predicament that ignores his social situation is not talk about man as he really is. And if the doctrine of the atonement shows the way of man's salvation from that predicament in the world, that too has to vary not merely in its imagery but in its fundamental content as well. Thus the truth itself that has to be affirmed about man, and not merely its expression, can be seen as something that changes with the changing character of man's social environment. And those changes bring in their train changes in what is rightly to be affirmed about the saving activity of God.

If the approach of these last paragraphs be accepted, we would have to acknowledge that what Christians affirm (and not merely how they affirm it) is substantially affected by the culture and by the society in which they find themselves. Can we admit that without thereby reducing theology to a second-hand reflection of the changing aspirations of society? Is the theologian doomed to become no more than an ineffective camp-follower in the wake of the genuinely creative social pioneer? The dangers are not to be underestimated. Was it not precisely readiness for adaptation to the contemporary social situation that made possible the support of the German Christians for the Nazi régime? But the difficulties though real are not insuperable, provided we insist, as I have already given reason for insisting, that while what the theologian says is rightly influenced by these sociological factors, it need not and should not be wholly determined by them. Other factors are also involved, in particular the facticity of the Christian past to which I referred at the end of the last section. To that we must now turn.

3. HISTORY

We have already given a good deal of attention to the impact of historical study on theology since it underlies the theologian's approach to the study both of the Bible and of church history that we surveyed earlier. Nevertheless it is so fundamental to the work of theology as a whole that it merits further discussion. Although in popular thought the nineteenth century is particularly renowned for the conflict of science and religion, the development of historical study in that century was of even more far-reaching importance for theology. Moreover in the last section we have seen that the theologian needs to be able to act as a genuinely dialectical partner with the psychologist and the sociologist and not just as a pale echo of them. The factual character of the Christian past and especially the facts concerning Jesus may have an important rôle to play in this respect.

The philosophy of history is a comparatively new study and there is little agreement between scholars in their attempts to analyze at a theoretical level what is implied by the way historians set about their task. But in practice there is a much wider agreement than the theoretical discussions might suggest about what actually constitutes doing history in a responsible and scholarly way. I want to stress at the outset some very general features that seem to me characteristic of the work of modern historians and which are of importance for the theologian in his consideration of the relation of historical knowledge to Christian theology. Much earlier historical writing was a form of apologetic or of propaganda for a particular cause of the historian's own day. It was specifically designed to show the past as leading up to and justifying certain institutions or desired changes of the moment. Critical study aims, and in no small measure succeeds, in separating history from propaganda. This involves two seemingly, but not ultimately, incompatible attitudes on the part of the historian. If he is to understand the past he has to do so in the first instance from within its own categories and its own presuppositions. If he imposes upon it too readily his own later terms of reference, he will be in danger of distorting what he sees. Yet in making his critical assessment of the past, he must work with and judge by his own contemporary understanding of how the world works. Moreover he has to acknowledge that he himself has a particular point of view which is bound to have an effect on the judgements that he makes. He must make every effort to eliminate bias, while also recognizing that there is no such thing as a purely neutral standpoint.

These considerations are of special importance to the Christian theologian, precisely because it is a fundamental feature of traditional Christian faith to see in its past history, and in the history of Jesus in particular, the determinative and distinctive element in that faith. When Christianity is spoken of as a 'historical' religion, this means something more than the obvious fact that Christianity has a history— every religion has that; it means that Christianity sees itself as rooted in history in a unique way. The point was put forcefully by Eric Mascall in his inaugural lecture as Professor of Historical Theology at King's College, London:

It has often been emphasized that Christianity is historical in a sense in which no other religion is, for it stands or falls by certain events which are alleged to have taken place during a particular period of forty-eight hours in Palestine nearly two thousand years ago.[1]

A Christianity which understands itself in these terms is bound to be particularly vulnerable to changes in historical understanding. Before discussing how the development of

---

[1] Quoted by A. R. Vidler, 'Historical Objections' in ed. Mackinnon, Williams, Vidler, and Bezzant, *Objections to Christian Belief* (London, 1963), p. 58. Two of the quotations that follow are drawn from the same essay.

historical study has impinged on these central issues of Christian faith, I want to consider first some more general challenges to any account of Christianity as a historical religion in this unique sense.

As in the case of science and religion, there are those who would argue that there is no essential relation between the two. Religion, it is said, is concerned with eternal truth and the contingent particularities of history cannot therefore be of vital importance to it. This position has not often been affirmed from within the mainstream of Christian tradition, but it has been held by men of deep religious insight and with a fundamental sympathy towards Christianity. Thus Tolstoy spoke of the supposition or probability that Christ never existed as 'like the destruction of the last outwork exposed to the enemy's attack, in order that the fortress (the moral teaching of goodness, which flows not from any one source in time or space, but from the whole spiritual life of humanity in its entirety) may remain impregnable'.[1] Gandhi declared in somewhat similar vein:

I may say that I have never been interested in an historical Jesus. I should not care if it was proved by someone that the man called Jesus never lived, and that what was narrated in the Gospels was a figment of the writer's imagination. For the Sermon on the Mount would still be true for me.[2]

But Christianity is more than a set of truths or even a set of injunctions for the good life. It is concerned with lived experience in its wholeness. It is certainly not absurd therefore to suggest that a life and not just truths or ideas should be of crucial importance for it. The difference between the two approaches can be illustrated from a contrast between mathematics and literature. In his attractive little book, *A Mathematician's Apology*, G. H. Hardy wrote:

Archimedes will be remembered when Aeschylus is forgotten because languages die and mathematical ideas do not.

C. P. Snow, in his edition of the book, appends the following comment:

[1] See A. Maude, *Life of Tolstoy* (Oxford, 1930), Vol. II, p. 51.
[2] See A. R. Vidler, op. cit., p. 59.

Even if we grant that 'Archimedes will be remembered when Aeschylus is forgotten' is not mathematical fame a little too anonymous to be wholly satisfying? We could form a fairly coherent picture of Aeschylus (still more of course of Shakespeare and Tolstoi) from their works alone, while Archimedes and Eudoxus would remain mere names.[1]

In the case of literature or of historical institutions the author or founder is related to that which he creates in a different way from that in which the mathematician is related to the truths that he discovers. The literary or historical pioneer cannot so easily be separated out from his achievements and left wholly out of account.

The analogies of course are imperfect. They do not remove all the sense of puzzlement that many find in the absolute link with history which Christianity has traditionally affirmed. But I think they do enough to show that it cannot simply be dismissed as absurd.

But the traditional account of Christianity's grounding in history may be called in question on somewhat different grounds. History, it has been argued, cannot be vital to religious faith, for history can never provide the certainty that religion demands. The point was made in vigorous style by Lessing in the eighteenth century. He insisted that however reliable a historical report might be, yet no historical truth could be demonstrated as certain. So if no historical truth could be demonstrated, nothing that was dependent on historical evidence could properly be believed with the absoluteness that religious faith demanded.

Lessing spoke as if the historical evidence concerning Jesus took us as near to certainty as historical evidence in the nature of the case was ever able to do. If he were to be taken at his face value, it would not be too difficult to retort that historical evidence can lead to a moral certainty which would be adequate to the needs of faith. But Lessing was writing with his tongue in his cheek. The historical evidence about Jesus is not of that kind. To some people, who would regard the kind of moral certainty of which I have spoken as

[1] G. H. Hardy, *A Mathematician's Apology* (Cambridge, 1967), pp. 21 and 93.

a sufficient basis for religious faith, it has appeared to fall well below the required level. Lowes Dickinson for example wrote:

My difficulty about Christianity is and always has been that Christians make the centre of their faith the historical existence of a man at a certain age. I dare say he *did* exist, though that has been doubted. But if he *did*, what was he really like? I cannot think religion can depend on such uncertainties.[1]

In suggesting that doubts about the historical existence of Jesus need to be taken seriously, Lowes Dickinson's statement errs almost as much in the direction of scepticism as Lessing's ironical remarks did in the opposite direction. But it does clarify the basic issue at stake. It would be absurd to suggest that for faith to be vitally linked to history, the relevant historical evidence would need to be such as to provide certain proof beyond all possibility of doubt for in the strictest sense of those words historical evidence can never do that. But it would be equally absurd to suggest that there could be a vital link, if the relevant historical evidence was almost wholly inconclusive. So the application of critical historical study to the basic events of Christian history poses this question: How confidently can we determine the basic historical issues? What measure of uncertainty is involved? Is it of such a kind that it undermines the reasonableness of understanding Christianity as an historical religion in the strong sense of which we have been speaking? I want to approach these questions by means of a brief survey of the way in which historical scholarship has dealt with the history of Jesus over the last hundred years, and then by a short discussion of the questions involved in a historical approach.

Schweitzer's famous book, *The Quest of the Historical Jesus*, was first published in 1906. It surveyed the results of the application of historical method to the life of Jesus which had been pursued with such rigour by nineteenth-century German scholarship. Its basic verdict was that the quest had failed in its attempt 'to strip from Him the robes of splendour with which He had been apparelled and to clothe Him once more

[1] A. R. Vidler, op. cit, p. 59.

with the coarse garments in which He had once walked in Galilee'. It failed primarily in Schweitzer's judgement because of men's intimate involvement, whether of love or hate, with the figure of Jesus. 'Each successive epoch of theology found its own thoughts in Jesus'; indeed 'each individual created Him in accordance with his own character'.[1]

But it was not only the problem of the objectivity of the scholar that lay behind the failure of the quest. It was also the problem of the nature of the sources. The gospels were not designed to present a history of Jesus. Historians are of course used to finding answers to their questions from sources which were not written with that purpose in view. But the historian cannot provide answers where there is no appropriate evidence to hand. The gospels, it came to be argued, were a form of preaching rather than of history. The most that the historical scholar could rightly hope to achieve was to clarify the preached message of the early Church. It was not possible for him to go behind that and present a reliable account of Jesus' actual life and ministry.

This line of approach was strongly developed in the work of Rudolf Bultmann. At one point he expressed the negative pole of his position in these words: 'I do indeed think that we can now know almost nothing concerning the life and personality of Jesus.'[2] Such a sceptical view of the possibilities of any firm knowledge about Jesus could only be combined with a positively Christian religious position by accepting a far greater separation between history and faith than has normally been characteristic of Christian theology. This Bultmann did. He argued for example that faith in Jesus was independent of the question whether or not Jesus called himself Messiah, for 'only the historian can answer this question—as far as it can be answered at all—and faith, being personal decision, cannot be dependent on a historian's labour'.[3] For Bultmann the historical questions about Jesus were largely unanswerable. But they were also

[1] A. Schweitzer, *Quest of the Historical Jesus* (London, 1911), pp. 4–5.

[2] R. Bultmann, *Jesus and the Word* (London, 1957), p. 8.

[3] Ibid., *Theology of the New Testament*, Vol. 1 (London, 1952), p. 26.

largely irrelevant. They had to be if faith was to be freely
personal faith and not dependent upon the erudite researches
of the historical scholar, without which no confident historical judgements could properly be made. Bultmann had no
desire to free man's faith from the authoritarian control of
ecclesiastical tradition only to submit it instead to the papacy
of the scholar.

But the reaction was too extreme. Bultmann hardly seems
to do justice to the nature of the New Testament material.
The New Testament writers did not of course seek to establish
the facts about Jesus by modern historical methods. But it
was a real historical figure who was at the heart of their
message, as passages like the opening section of 1 Corinthians
15 bear witness. If our faith today is to be faith that concerns
Jesus and that takes him with equal historical seriousness as a
historical figure, it is hard to see how we can avoid taking the
historical questions seriously.

So there was a swing back of the pendulum, marked particularly by an occasion in 1953 at a gathering of Bultmann's
former pupils when Ernst Käsemann declared the necessity
for a new quest of the historical Jesus. With improved critical
tools and less ambitious goals the 'new questers' hoped to be
able to overcome the shortcomings of the old. But it is questionable how far they have in fact succeeded in doing so. In
the eyes of some of their critics at least they were not wholly
liberated from the old tendency to create Jesus in the image
of their own epoch. 'We smile today', wrote Prigent, 'at the
humanistic portrait of Jesus which the nineteenth century
painted. But do you think that the same smile will not rise on
the lips of those who detect tomorrow, in certain recent works,
Jesus the existentialist?'[1] Moreover while the sources at our
disposal certainly provide sufficient leads to make possible
reasoned suggestion about the nature of Jesus' life and ministry, yet the radical differences between the various accounts
put forward by responsible scholars, with good evidence to
support them in each case, suggest that that evidence is not

[1] Quoted by J. M. Robinson, *A New Quest of the Historical Jesus* (London,
1959), p. 76.

such as to bring us anywhere near the level of moral certainty.

But the life of Jesus has never been thought of as uniformly important for faith. Most important of all is his resurrection from the dead. Can this be substantiated by historical enquiry? Or shown at least to be a reasonable belief in the light of a critical handling of the historical evidence? The question raises special problems for the historian because of the uniqueness of that which is being affirmed. There is a weak sense of the word 'unique' in which every historical happening is unique. Each event is unrepeatable and has no identical twin. But this does not of course disturb the historian or prevent him assessing the probability of the event having happened in some particular way. The resurrection is unique in a much stronger sense. It is different in kind from any other historical happening. Even in other accounts of raising from the dead like Lazarus or Jairus' daughter, the person raised returns to his old kind of life to die again in due time; Jesus passes through death to a new kind of life. Yet historical enquiry is clearly relevant. The historian can properly discuss the evidence for the empty tomb, the accounts of appearances to the disciples, the transformation in the disciples themselves and the way in which the resurrection figures not only as the central element but as the distinctive *raison d'être* of the earliest preaching. He may come to the conclusion that it is difficult to offer any explanation of these—or at least of some of them—which is itself free from serious difficulty. But this does not in itself justify him in going on to assert the resurrection as historically probable. The historian is not unused to finding himself faced with puzzling phenomena which the evidence available does not enable him to explain satisfactorily. But it is fundamental to his method as a historian that he discounts the possibility of the wholly miraculous. If he did not, it would be impossible for him to assess historical probabilities consistently. For to do that he has to asume a general consistency in the way the world behaves. He need not be affirming the absolute impossibility of the miraculous. He can hardly avoid insisting on the absolute exclusion of its possibility from his work as a historian. In the face of this

basic feature of historical method, whatever may ultimately
be affirmed about the resurrection, it cannot be regarded as
a well-attested fact on general historical grounds, indepen-
dently accessible, as it were, to provide a firm foundation on
which the superstructure of Christian faith may then be
built.

Historical work concerning Jesus and the resurrection
continues. Its results, as I have stressed, are very varied.
But if the general lineaments of the relation of history to
theology are as I have tried to describe them with the help
of these examples, then what implications does this have
for the work of Christian theology? Certainly the relation of
faith to history needs to be seen as more problematical than
the citation from Professor Mascall would suggest. Neither
the history of Jesus nor evidence for the resurrection provides
a firm substratum of fact which points inexorably in the
direction of supernatural belief. History does not contribute
as decisively to Christian faith as that kind of an account
would suggest.

In our earlier discussion of philosophical arguments for the
existence of God, I argued that the arguments did not work
as clear proofs of theistic faith, but that it was possible to use
some of the insights embodied in those traditional arguments
as part of a lesser kind of cumulative case for the reasonableness of theism. The rôle of historical evidence for Christian
belief is somewhat similar. It is not decisive. It cannot be the
starting-point of any tight argument for the truth of the
Christian faith. There is an ambivalence about the history of
Jesus and about the history of the Church which is comparable to the ambivalence of evidence from the natural world.
Much theological work is rightly devoted to clarifying the
nature of the historical evidence. But those historical studies
cannot be looked to to do away with that ambivalence in a
direction either favourable or hostile to Christian faith as a
whole.

Historical study has been a dominating aspect of theological work for the last hundred years. The full significance
of that study for the structure of theology as a whole has still
to be assimilated. It certainly cannot provide a firm initial

grounding for Christian theology. It should be seen rather as providing one more, very important, motif within the theologian's attempt to interpret the world as a whole. In the past it has often appeared to be a motif of overriding importance. It will always remain of importance, but in course of time some of the other aspects of the theologian's work, that we have also considered, may come to assume more closely comparable measures of importance.

Conclusion:

The Theologian at Work

We have looked at the main sub-sections of theological study and considered the implications of other related disciplines. Is it possible to draw together the threads of the discussion and answer the initial question: what is theology?

Before attempting a direct answer to that question, I want to suggest the shape that an answer might be expected to take by considering how such a question might be answered in terms of another discipline. Imagine a Freudian psychologist faced with the question: what is Freudian psychology? His answer, I suggest, might move through three stages. It would probably start descriptively. Anyone wanting to understand Freudian psychology would have to undertake a variety of specific studies—the life and writings of Freud himself, what later Freudians have made of his ideas in the light of subsequent reflection and further experience, philosophical assumptions implicit in these ideas and their practical outworking in therapy. Then as a second stage it would be possible for him to attempt to give, on the basis of those various specific studies, a coherent account of the way in which the human mind and human behaviour were understood to function. But there would certainly be more than one way of doing that. Some answers might take Freud's own position as fundamental and see later thought as providing no more than minor additions or corrections. Others, while acknowledging the pioneering position of Freud's own work, might regard some later theorists with the benefit of their further experience as better able to provide the outline of a satisfactory unified account. Moreover other accounts would vary as to which of Freud's ideas was given the more dominant rôle when bringing the various aspects of his thought into a coherent whole. Finally our Freudian psychologist might be challenged to declare whether this was simply a way in which he chose to regard man, something to which he would remain committed irrespective of whatever evidence might emerge from other psychological schools or in the world at large. He would be hardly likely to claim that it was a purely private, privileged system of knowledge. But in calling himself a Freudian he would at the very least be expressing the conviction that its basic insights were not fundamentally mistaken. Further knowledge, deriving from the work of other psychologists, of biochemists or of sociologists, might demand substantial modifications in the future. Their form and their extent could not be foretold in advance. But however great, they would, in his expectation, be likely to constitute not a refutation but rather a clarification of the basic insights embodied in Freudian psychology.

Let me now set out a possible answer to the question, 'What is Christian theology?', that follows the same three stages. No satisfactory answer can be given that does not begin descriptively with the various, relatively discrete studies that theology includes—the Bible with its record of the coming of Christ, of all that led up to that coming and of the first response of faith to it: the history of the Church as the record of how that response has been continued in the lives and beliefs of men down the ages: the philosophical assumptions that are implicit in the acceptance of that faith as true, and the practical application in worship and in ethics.

But theology is more than the sum of these separate studies. It seeks to bring them together into a coherent understanding of the world as the object of God's creative activity and redemptive love in Christ. As in the case of Freudian psychology there are many different ways in which that unifying task can be done. For some the words and life of Christ hold a controlling position and all that comes later is no more than subsidiary clarification. Others may give greater priority to subsequent developments which have tested and revised their understanding of the faith in the light of later experience, seeing in them that fuller truth into which the Holy

Spirit is said to lead the Church after the time of Jesus. Again some may treat the categories of creation and redemption as distinct and contrasting moments in God's work in the world; others will present a scheme in which they belong far more closely together as one continuing pattern of divine activity. Here criteria for preferring one scheme to another are difficult to find, and it is easy for prejudice or tradition to rule men's decisions unchecked. Criteria are certainly of a very loose kind, but rational discussion of the issue is possible. It is possible, for example, to assess the relative internal coherence of different schemes of thought and also the degrees of their consistency with other areas of knowledge.

For the second stage of our answer merges inevitably into the third. Is Christian theology simply a way in which certain people, called Christians, choose to interpret their experience? Or is it open to modification by the insights of other religions and of other forms of knowledge? The issue at stake is in the end a matter of degree. The idea of a Christian theology which could ignore the findings of all other disciplines is both theoretically absurd and practically impossible. Yet there must be special evidence of special importance, if the subject is to exist at all. It is a question of the degree of distinctiveness or discontinuity involved in the work of theology. That is a problem which, I have argued, arises in relation to any particular discipline. Physics, psychology, sociology, history rightly have their own categories; they are neither identical with one another nor unrelated. So too with theology. It has its own categories and embodies insights which the Christian theologian is convinced will not turn out to be fundamentally mistaken. Throughout its history it has been modified by its contact with other studies. It has often been unaware of what has been happening to it or reluctant to accept the modifications that have been pressed upon it. Today it is more generally ready to acknowledge the way in which other disciplines impinge upon it. The nature of their interaction is fluid and may hold many surprises in store for the theologian in the future. But his task, though inevitably elusive because of the elusive nature of his subject-matter, is not likely to prove evanescent.

The variety of schemes which theologians in the past have put forward and still do today is partly the result of human error. At some points mistakes are learnt and can be corrected. But variety is not necessarily the fruit of error. For no theology can speak fully or directly about God. Some variety is appropriate and can be constructive. Different theologies may be complementary to one another rather than in competition. Such variety can help theology as a whole to move beyond that which any single scheme of theology by itself could achieve in pointing to the true object of all theological study, which is inexhaustibly greater than all faltering human understanding, namely God himself.

Bibliography

This book has ranged so widely that almost any work of theology—and a good many non-theological works as well—could qualify as 'further reading' to which it points. I shall not attempt to provide an outline bibliography for a standard course in Christian theology. My aim is rather to suggest a few books which carry a stage further the kinds of reflection about the value of theology that I have raised. The chief criterion of selection is that they are the books in that class which have particularly appealed to me.

I. Introduction

S. W. Sykes, *Christian Theology Today* (London, 1971) is not just one more outline of Christian theology, but a reflection on the nature of theological work with rather more attention to content than this book.

Religious experience is not something that easily lends itself to being written about. Rudolf Otto's *The Idea of the Holy* (Oxford, 1st ed. 1923; 2nd ed. 1950) is more lively than many more recent writings. J. Bowker, *The Sense of God* (Oxford, 1973) is a vigorous discussion of various proposed explanations of religious experience.

The relation of Christianity to other religions is well brought out in a book of essays, edited by John Hick, *Truth and Dialogue* (London, 1974) and the impact of such an approach on one man's Christian theology is clearly exemplified in John Hick's own collection of essays, *God and the Universe of Faiths* (London, 1973).

II. Christian Theology from the Inside.

The approaches of the various subjects within Christian

theology are described in F. G. Healey, ed., *Preface to Christian Studies* (London, 1971).

S.C.M. Centrebooks include two excellent short books giving lively accounts of contemporary critical approaches to the two testaments and the results to which they point— J. S. Bowden, *What about the Old Testament?* and T. G. A. Baker, *What is the New Testament?* (London, 1969). A larger book similarly bringing the New Testament and modern study of it to life is C. F. D. Moule, *The Birth of the New Testament* (London, 1962).

Church history is best taken further by getting into the history of a particular period in which one is interested. There is a reflective article 'On Method in Church History' by H. Willmer in *Theology*, Vol. LXXVII (April 1974), pp. 186–92.

Reflections on the method appropriate to doctrinal work appear in the opening sections of some of the most important theological writings of the age—e.g. in Vol. 1 of K. Barth's *Church Dogmatics*, P. Tillich's *Systematic Theology*, and K. Rahner's *Theological Investigations*. I have tried to work out the approach sketched here in relation to the early history of doctrine in my *Making of Christian Doctrine* (Cambridge, 1967) and in relation to contemporary doctrine in my *Remaking of Christian Doctrine* (London, 1974).

On philosophy of religion generally P. R. Baelz, *Christian Theology and Metaphysics* (London, 1968) provides a valuable reflective approach. H. D. Lewis, *Teach Yourself Philosophy of Religion* (London, 1968) is clear and comprehensive—rather more like the standard textbook than most of the other books listed. On the existence of God, the classical arguments are well illustrated in J. Hick, ed., *The Existence of God* (London, 1964) which gives a useful selection of extracts with a helpful introduction. A contemporary argument for theistic belief is well set out in B. Mitchell, *The Justification of Religious Belief* (London, 1973). On religious language, I. T. Ramsey, *Religious Language* (London, 1957) and F. W. Dillistone, ed., *Myth and Symbol* (London, 1960) are worth consulting.

III. The Impact of Other Studies.

'Religion and science' has given rise to many studies. Outstanding is Ian Barbour, *Issues in Science and Religion* (London,
1966). John Habgood, *Religion and Science* (London, 1964) is a
valuable treatment on a smaller scale.

Discussions of authority in religion are not so plentiful. A
wide range of attitudes found expression in two collections of
essays—J. M. Todd, ed., *Problems of Authority* (London, 1962),
an Anglo-French Roman Catholic Symposium, and R. R.
Williams, ed., *Authority and the Church* (London, 1965), the
report of a conference between theologians of the Church of
England and the German Evangelical Church.

On psychology and sociology, M. Argyle and B. Beit-
Hallahmi, *The Social Psychology of Religion* (London, 1975) and
R. Towler, *Homo Religiosus: Sociological Problems in the Study of
Religion* (London, 1974) give thorough general discussion of
recent work in those fields. P. Berger, *The Social Reality of
Religion* (London, 1969) gives a particularly valuable insight
into the way a sociological perspective may affect religious
and theological study.

V. A. Harvey, *The Historian and the Believer* (London, 1967)
is an outstanding discussion of the impact of critical historical
study on Christian theology. Its particular impact on recent
work on the person of Jesus is well described in H. Zahrnt,
The Historical Jesus (London, 1963).

Index